What A Life!

Stories of Amazing People

Longman

Milada Broukal

What A Life! Stories of Amazing People, Beginning

Pearson Education, 10 Bank Street, White Plains, NY 10606

Editorial director: Allen Ascher
Executive editor: Louisa Hellegers
Acquisition editor: Laura Le Dréan
Development manager: Penny Laporte
Development editor: Andrea Bryant, James Morgan, Cheryl Pavik
Director of design and production: Rhea Banker
Associate director of electronic production: Aliza Greenblatt
Managing editor: Linda Moser
Production supervisor: Liza Pleva
Production editor: Martin Yu
Senior manufacturing manager: Patrice Fraccio
Manufacturing supervisor: Edith Pullman
Photo research: Marianne Carello
Cover design: Elizabeth Carlson
Cover credits: Mountain climber: Solstice Photography/Artville; Violinist: Eye Wire Photography; Soccer
    ball/player: Eye Wire Photography; Writer: Eye Wire Photography; Scientist: Michael Stuckey/Comstock
Text design: Elizabeth Carlson
Text composition: Publication Services, Inc.
Photo credits: p. 1, Archive Photos; p. 5, Art Resource, N.Y.; p. 9, © Bettmann/CORBIS; p. 13, © Bettmann/CORBIS;
    p. 17, Tony Stone Images; p. 21, CORBIS; p. 25, A'Lelia Bundles/Walker Family Collection; p. 29, A/P Wide World
    Photos; p. 33, © Bettmann/CORBIS; p. 37, London Daily Express/Archive Photos; p. 41, A/P Wide World Photos;
    p. 45, A/P Wide World Photos; p. 49, © Bettmann/CORBIS; p. 53, Imapress /Archive Photos; p. 57, © Bettmann/
    CORBIS; p. 61, AP/Wide World Photos; p. 65, Anne Frank House; p. 69, AP/Wide World Photos; p. 73, © Photo by
    Michael Neugebauer; p. 77, AP/Wide World Photos; p. 81, AP/Wide World Photos; p. 85, Matrix International, Inc.;
    p. 89, AP/Wide World Photos; p. 93, © Hulton-Deutsch Collection/CORBIS; p. 97, Cynthia Johnson/Liaison
    Agency, Inc.

Library of Congress Cataloging-in-Publication Data

Broukal, Milada.
    What a life! stories of amazing people / by Milada Broukal.
        p.   cm.
    Contents: Beginning
    ISBN: 0-201-61996-2
    1. English language—Textbooks for foreign speakers.   2. Biography—
Problems, exercises, etc.   3. Readers—Biography.   I. Title.

PE1128.B716   2000
428.6'4—dc21   99-059443

11 12 13 14 15 16 17—VH—12 11 10 09 08

CONTENTS

INTRODUCTION

What A Life! Stories of Amazing People is a beginning reader. It is the first in a three-book series of biographies for students of English as a second or foreign language. Twenty-five people have been selected for this book: 13 women and 12 men. Their backgrounds and talents are very different, ranging from a nineteenth-century Russian composer, to an African American boxing champion, to a young Chinese artist. All of them have made significant contributions to the world.

Each unit focuses on one person's biography. The biographies have been arranged in chronological order; however, they can be taught in any order.

Each unit contains:

• A prereading activity
• A reading passage (300–350 words)
• Topic-related vocabulary work
• Comprehension exercises, including pair work
• Discussion questions
• A writing activity

BEFORE YOU READ opens with a picture of the person featured in that unit. Prereading questions follow. Their purpose is to motivate students to read, encourage predictions about the content of the reading, and involve the students' own experiences when possible. Vocabulary can be presented as the need arises.

The **READING** passage should be first done individually, by skimming for the general content. The teacher may wish to explain the bolded vocabulary words at this point. The students should then do a second, closer reading. Further reading(s) can be done aloud.

The two **VOCABULARY** exercises focus on the bolded words in the reading. *Meaning*, a definition exercise, encourages students to work out the meanings from the context. The second exercise, *Use*, reinforces the vocabulary further by making students use the words in a meaningful, yet possibly different, context. This section can be done during or after the reading phase, or both.

There are several **COMPREHENSION** exercises. Each unit contains *Understanding the Reading* and *Remembering Details*. These are followed by either *Understanding the Sequence* or *Sentence Completion*. All confirm the content of the text either in general or in detail. These exercises for developing reading skills can be done individually, in pairs, in small groups, or as a class. It is preferable to do these exercises in conjunction with the text, since they are not meant to test memory. *Understanding the Sequence* is followed by *Tell the Story*, and *Sentence Completion* is followed by *Dictation*. Both exercises involve spoken pair work. In each case, students can correct each other's mistakes.

DISCUSSION questions encourage students to bring their own ideas and imagination to the related topics in each reading. They can also provide insights into cultural similarities and differences.

WRITING provides the stimulus for students to write simple sentences about their own lives. Teachers should use their own discretion when deciding whether or not to correct the writing exercises.

What A Life! is an exciting introduction to some of history's most amazing people. Teachers may want to support their discussions with other books, magazine and newspaper articles, or videos. There are also many good websites, three of which are listed below. These sites are very informative, yet easy to navigate. They will be excellent resources for students and teachers alike.

www.encarta.com is a general, online encyclopedia.

www.biography.com is a website that specializes in biographies.

www.pathfinder.com/time/time100.com features profiles of *Time* magazine's choices for the "100 Most Important People of the 20th Century." Several of the people in this book—Albert Einstein, Pablo Picasso, Akio Morita, Anne Frank, Muhammad Ali, Pelé, and Princess Diana—were among those that were chosen.

UNIT 1

WILLIAM SHAKESPEARE

(1564–1616)

BEFORE YOU READ

William Shakespeare was a very famous writer. What do you know about him? Are these sentences true? Check (✔) *Yes* or *No*.

	Yes	No
1. Shakespeare was American.	○ Yes	○ No
2. Shakespeare wrote poems and plays.	○ Yes	○ No
3. He was an actor.	○ Yes	○ No
4. His plays are still popular today.	○ Yes	○ No

Now read about William Shakespeare and check your answers.

WILLIAM SHAKESPEARE

At the age of one, William Shakespeare was **lucky** to be alive. After he was born, a deadly **disease** came to England. It was called the plague. It killed thousands of people. But William Shakespeare lived.

Shakespeare grew up in Stratford-upon-Avon, England. He went to school nine hours a day, six days a week. In 1582, at age 18, he married Anne Hathaway, a farmer's daughter. She was eight years older than he was. Their first child was a daughter. Later they had **twins.** In 1585, Shakespeare left Stratford-upon-Avon. His wife and children stayed behind. No one knows why he left or what he did between 1585 and 1592.

In 1592, Shakespeare lived in London. He rented rooms or lived with friends. He visited his wife and family once a year. Shakespeare became an actor, and he also wrote **plays.** He usually acted in his own plays. Some of his most famous plays were *Romeo and Juliet, Hamlet,* and *Macbeth.* He wrote 37 plays in all. They are still popular today.

Then the plague came again. Many people died. The theaters closed for two years. Shakespeare could not write plays, so he wrote **poems**. When the theaters opened, Shakespeare wrote plays again. Shakespeare had a theater group. It was the most successful group of that time. Shakespeare earned almost no money from his writing. But he made a lot of money from acting. With this money he bought a large house in Stratford-upon-Avon for his family. He was friendly with the richest people in town. He was a gentleman—a man of high class who didn't have to work.

At age 49, Shakespeare **retired** and went to live in Stratford-upon-Avon. He died at 52. He left his money to his family. He left his **genius** to the world.

VOCABULARY

◆ MEANING

Write the correct words in the blanks.

disease	twins	plays	lucky
retired	genius	poems	

1. William Shakespeare had good fortune. Other babies died, but he did not. He was ___lucky___.

2. The plague was a terrible _____. It was a sickness that passed from one person to another.

3. Shakespeare wrote _____, and he and his friends acted in them at the theater.

4. Shakespeare wrote very well. He had a special ability. He was a _____.

5. Shakespeare got older. He stopped working and _____.

6. Shakespeare's wife had two children born at the same time. She had
   _____.

7. Shakespeare wrote about ideas and emotions. The writing had short lines and
   few words. He wrote _____.

◆ USE

Work with a partner to answer these questions. Use complete sentences.

1. What is your *lucky* number?

2. The plague is a *disease*. What are two other diseases?

3. *Hamlet* is a *play*. What is the name of another famous play?

4. Who do you think is a *genius?*

5. What do *twins* have that is the same?

6. What does a person do when he or she *retires?*

COMPREHENSION

◆ UNDERSTANDING THE READING

Circle the letter of the correct answer.

1. Shakespeare worked _____.
   a. in Stratford-upon-Avon   b. in London   c. near his family

2. When the theaters closed, Shakespeare _____.
   a. wrote plays   b. started a theater group   c. wrote poems

3. Shakespeare made his money from his _____.
   a. acting   b. poems   c. plays

◆ REMEMBERING DETAILS

Reread the passage and answer the questions.

1. At what age did Shakespeare marry?

2. Where did Shakespeare's family live?

3. How many plays did Shakespeare write?

4. What are two plays that Shakespeare wrote?

5. Where did Shakespeare go when he retired?

6. Who did he leave his money to?

◆ UNDERSTANDING THE SEQUENCE

Which happened first? Write 1 on the line. Which happened second? Write 2 on the line.

1. _____ There was a plague in England.
   _____ William Shakespeare was born.

2. _____ Shakespeare had twins.
   _____ Shakespeare had a daughter.

3. _____ Shakespeare went to London.
   _____ Shakespeare married.

4. _____ Shakespeare bought a large house in Stratford-upon-Avon.
   _____ Shakespeare retired.

◆ TELL THE STORY

Work with a partner. Tell the story of William Shakespeare to your partner. Use your own words. Your partner can ask you questions about the story. Then, your partner tells you the story and you ask questions.

DISCUSSION

Discuss the answers to these questions with your classmates.

1. Do you know any of Shakespeare's plays? Which one(s)?

2. Why do you think Shakespeare's plays have been popular for over 400 years?

3. Do you want to be an actor or actress? Why or why not?

WRITING

Write about a movie you saw.

Example: *I saw a movie. The name of the movie was* Titanic. *It was about a famous ship.*

_____

_____

_____

_____

UNIT 2
LOUIS XIV
(1638–1715)

BEFORE YOU READ

Louis XIV was a famous French king. What do you know about kings and queens? Answer the questions with a partner.

1. How does a person become a king or queen?
2. Do any countries have kings or queens today?
3. What do you think of when you think of a king or queen?
4. Look at the picture of Louis XIV. What can you say about him?

Now read about Louis XIV.

LOUIS XIV

Louis became King of France at the age of five when his father died. In the beginning, he was too young to **rule,** so his mother helped him. Then at age 17, Louis ruled the country alone. He was king for 72 years. France became a **powerful** country with Louis as king. But Louis lived a life of **luxury,** which made people angry.

Louis built a huge **palace** at Versailles, near Paris. It took 40 years to finish it. At one time, 36,000 people worked on building the palace. The palace cost so much money that Louis did not let people talk about it. The gardens of the palace had 1,400 **fountains.** The fountains used a lot of water so they worked for only three hours at a time.

The fountains used water, but Louis did not! He hated to wash. He took only three baths in his life. He washed only one part of his body—the **tip** of the nose. Everyone in the palace had to do what the king did, so people washed only their noses!

Louis XIV had other unusual rules. He liked to keep the windows open at the palace. He wanted dozens of people around him when he got dressed. Also, only the king and queen could sit on chairs with arms. Everybody else had to sit on chairs with no arms.

Louis had problems sleeping. People say that he had 413 beds. He went from one bed to another until he fell asleep. But he had a good **appetite.** A normal dinner for Louis was four bowls of soup, two whole chickens, ham, lamb, a salad, cakes, fruit, and hard-boiled eggs. He also drank a lot of champagne because his doctor told him to. He lived to be 77 years old. When he died, doctors said his stomach was two times the size of a normal stomach.

Louis XIV was not always popular, but he was an important king in the history of France. He was so important that he was called "the Sun King."

VOCABULARY

◆ MEANING

Write the correct words in the blanks.

rule	powerful	luxury	palace
fountains	appetite	tip	

1. Louis XIV built a very large house called Versailles. It was a beautiful

   _____.

2. A king's job is to _____ his country.

3. When Louis XIV was king, his country was very important. It was a

   _____ country.

4. Louis liked to have very expensive things. These things were not necessary.

   He liked _____.

5. Louis always ate big dinners. He had a good _____.

6. In a park, water often comes out of _____.

7. The end of your nose is the _____ of it.

◆ USE

Work with a partner to answer these questions. Use complete sentences.

1. Who *rules* England today?

2. What comes out of a *fountain?*

3. Who are some people who live a life of *luxury?*

4. Who is a *powerful* person?

5. What is the name of a famous *palace?*

COMPREHENSION

◆ UNDERSTANDING THE READING

Circle the letter of the correct answer.

1. Louis XIV was a famous king because _____.

   a. he ate a lot   b. he washed only   c. he built the palace
                          his nose   of Versailles

2. Louis XIV loved _____.

   a. beautiful beds   b. a life of luxury   c. baths

3. Louis XIV ruled _____.

   a. for a long time   b. in England   c. 36,000 people

◆ REMEMBERING DETAILS

Reread the passage and answer the questions.

1. How long was Louis XIV king?

2. How old was Louis XIV when he ruled the country alone?

3. What was the name of Louis's palace?

4. How many fountains were there in the gardens of the palace?

5. What part of his body did Louis wash?

6. In the palace, who sat on chairs with arms?

Match the words in Column A and Column B to make sentences.

A	B
___ 1. Louis liked	a. sleep well.
___ 2. Louis hated	b. a good appetite.
___ 3. Louis had	c. to keep the windows open.
___ 4. Louis didn't	d. when he was 17 years old.
___ 5. Louis became king	e. when he was five years old.
___ 6. Louis ruled the country alone	f. to wash.

◆ DICTATION

Work with a partner. Read four sentences from the exercise above. Your partner listens and writes the sentences. Then, your partner reads four sentences, and you write them.

DISCUSSION

Discuss the answers to these questions with your classmates.

1. Long ago, people didn't take many baths or showers. How often should you wash? Once or twice a day? Once a week? Give reasons.

2. Louis had a lot of unusual rules about the way he lived. Do you know someone that has unusual rules? Describe them.

3. Would you like to live a life like Louis XIV? Why or why not?

WRITING

Write about what you eat on a normal day.

Example: *In the morning I have toast and coffee for breakfast.*

_____

_____

_____

_____

UNIT 3

FLORENCE NIGHTINGALE
(1820–1910)

BEFORE YOU READ

Florence Nightingale was a famous nurse. What are three important qualities for a nurse? Discuss your answers with a partner.

A nurse should be:

clean	kind	educated	strong
rich	pretty	intelligent	polite

Now read about Florence Nightingale.

FLORENCE NIGHTINGALE

Florence Nightingale was English, but she was born in Italy. Her parents named her Florence, after the city. Her family was rich, so Florence grew up with everything she wanted. When she became a young woman, her parents wanted her to get married. But Florence did not want to get married. She wanted to be a **nurse.** Her parents were angry. In those days, hospitals were dirty places. **Respectable** women did not work in hospitals. But Florence did not listen to her parents. She studied to be a nurse. Soon, she **supervised** a hospital for women in London. She was a great success.

In 1854, there was a war. Many British soldiers were in a hospital in Turkey. The hospital needed help. Florence Nightingale **volunteered** to go to Turkey. She brought 38 nurses to help her. When she got there, 42 percent of the soldiers in the hospital were dying. The hospital was very dirty. There was not enough food or clothing for the sick. Nightingale and her nurses started to clean and put the hospital in order. In just one month only 2 percent of the soldiers were dying! Nightingale worked 20 hours a day. Every night she walked around the hospital with her **lamp.** She **comforted** the sick soldiers. The soldiers loved her. They called her the "Lady with the Lamp." Her story was in the newspapers in England, and she became famous. Even Queen Victoria, the queen of England, wanted to meet her.

After two years, Nightingale went back to England. She was very sick, but she still worked. She started a school for nurses. The school continues to this day. Nightingale never married. But she did not live alone. She had 60 cats. When she was 43, Nightingale became sick. She was in bed for the rest of her life. She continued to work to help others. She died at age 90. We remember Florence Nightingale because she helped make nursing the important **profession** that it is today.

VOCABULARY

◆ MEANING

Write the correct words in the blanks.

nurse	respectable	supervised	volunteered
lamp	comforted	profession	

1. Florence Nightingale wanted to take care of the sick. She wanted to be a

   _____.

2. Nightingale came from a good family. She was a _____ young woman.

3. Nightingale asked to go to Turkey. She _____ to go.

4. At night Nightingale carried a _____ to help her see in the dark.

5. Nightingale made the soldiers feel better and less sad. She _____ them.

6. Nightingale told other nurses what to do. She _____ them.

7. Before Florence Nightingale, you did not need special education to be a nurse. Nursing was not a _____.

◆ USE

Work with a partner to answer these questions. Use complete sentences.

1. Nursing is a *profession*. What are three other professions? What profession do you want to work in?

2. What does a *nurse* do?

3. Nursing is a *respectable* job today. What are two other respectable jobs?

4. We are having a picnic Saturday afternoon. What do you *volunteer* to bring?

5. When you were a child, who *comforted* you when you were sick?

COMPREHENSION

◆ UNDERSTANDING THE READING

Circle the letter of the correct answer.

1. Florence Nightingale grew up and wanted to _____.
   a. be a respectable girl   b. be a nurse   c. get married

2. Nightingale was famous in England because she _____.
   a. helped sick soldiers   b. walked with a lamp   c. volunteered to go to Turkey

3. Nightingale is famous today because she _____.
   a. met the Queen   b. worked in a hospital   c. started the profession of nursing

◆ REMEMBERING DETAILS

One word in each sentence is not correct. Find the word and cross it out. Write the correct word.

1. Nightingale wanted to be a wife.

2. British soldiers were dying in a hospital in Florence.

3. Every night Nightingale walked in the hospital with her nurses.

4. Queen Elizabeth of England wanted to meet Nightingale.

5. Nightingale went back to England after five years in Turkey.

6. Nightingale died at the age of 43.

Which happened first? Write 1 on the line. Which happened second? Write 2 on the line.

1. _____ In 1854, there was a war.
   _____ Nightingale became a nurse.

2. _____ Nightingale worked 20 hours a day.
   _____ Nightingale went to Turkey.

3. _____ Nightingale became famous.
   _____ Newspapers wrote about Nightingale.

4. _____ Nightingale started a school for nurses.
   _____ Nightingale was in bed for the rest of her life.

◆ TELL THE STORY

Work with a partner. Tell the story of Florence Nightingale to your partner. Use your own words. Your partner can ask you questions about the story. Then, your partner tells you the story and you ask questions.

DISCUSSION

Discuss the answers to these questions with your classmates.

1. Imagine you are 18 years old and come from a very rich family. What do you want to do first? Explain your answer.

   look for a husband or wife   go to parties

   go to college   get a job

   help people   other

2. Do you want to be a nurse? Why or why not?

3. When you were a child, what did you want to be?

WRITING

Write about the profession of someone in your family.

Example: *My father is a taxi driver. He works 10 hours a day. He doesn't work on Sunday.*

_____

_____

_____

_____

UNIT 4

EMILY DICKINSON
(1830–1886)

BEFORE YOU READ

Emily Dickinson was a great poet. Look at her picture. What do you think about her? Are these sentences true? Check (✔) *Yes* or *No*.

1. Emily Dickinson was American.	○ Yes	○ No
2. She liked to be outside.	○ Yes	○ No
3. She liked to go to parties.	○ Yes	○ No
4. She wore expensive, fashionable clothes.	○ Yes	○ No
5. Emily Dickinson was happy.	○ Yes	○ No

Now read about Emily Dickinson and check your answers.

EMILY DICKINSON

Emily Dickinson was a very famous American poet. She wrote about 2,000 poems, but only four were published in her lifetime. No one wanted to **publish** her work because it was different from what other poets wrote. After Dickinson died, her poems were finally published. Then she became famous.

Some things about Emily Dickinson's life are strange and **mysterious.** She was born in 1830 in Amherst, Massachusetts, to a rich and well-known family. She had a brother and a sister. Emily was shy and quiet, but she had friends. She went to parties like other young girls her age and met young men. But she did not fall in love with any of them and never married.

After a while, Emily Dickinson did not want to see her friends. She stayed home. She read, worked in the **garden,** and wrote poetry. Dickinson wrote her poems everywhere. She wrote them on bits of newspaper or anything that was near. Later, she wrote them out carefully. When she was 28, something happened. Dickinson was very **upset.** No one knows why. Some people say she loved a married man. Others say she was unhappy because nobody wanted to publish her poetry. She continued to write anyway.

As she got older, Dickinson wanted to be alone more often. When someone came to the house, she ran upstairs to **hide.** For the last 16 years of her life, she never left her home. The curtains were always closed. She dressed only in white. One day Dickinson became **ill,** but she did not let the doctor in her room. He could only see her from the doorway.

Dickinson died at the age of 55. Her sister found her poems, and they were finally published. Sadly, Emily Dickinson did not live to enjoy her great success.

VOCABULARY

◆ MEANING

Write the correct words in the blanks.

publish	mysterious	garden
upset	hide	ill

1. Emily Dickinson was _____, so the doctor came.

2. Dickinson liked to go in her _____. She liked the flowers and plants outside of her house.

3. It is _____; we do not know the reason why Dickinson wore only white.

4. Dickinson was sad and angry. She was _____.

5. Dickinson wanted to _____ from visitors. She didn't want them to see or find her.

6. Dickinson wanted people to read her poems in books. She wanted to
   _____ them.

◆ USE

Work with a partner to answer these questions. Use complete sentences.

1. People *publish* poems. What else do they publish?

2. What things do you think are *mysterious?*

3. What makes you *upset?*

4. What do people sometimes *hide?*

5. When you are *ill,* what do you do?

COMPREHENSION

◆ UNDERSTANDING THE READING

Circle the letter of the correct answer.

1. Emily Dickinson _____.

   a. was famous before   b. was famous after   c. had a normal life
      she died   she died

2. Dickinson _____ all the time.

   a. visited friends   b. worked in her garden   c. wrote poems

3. In the last 16 years of her life, Dickinson _____.

   a. was ill all the time   b. did not leave   c. was happier
                                        her home   than before

◆ REMEMBERING DETAILS

Circle T if the sentence is true. Circle F if it is false.

	True	False
1. Dickinson had no friends when she was young.	T	F
2. Dickinson never married.	T	F
3. Dickinson dressed in white all her life.	T	F
4. Dickinson wrote more than 3,000 poems.	T	F
5. Dickinson's sister found the poems.	T	F
6. Dickinson came from a respectable family.	T	F

Which happened first? Write 1 on the line. Which happened second? Write 2 on the line.

1. _____ Dickinson did not want to see her friends.
   _____ Dickinson went to parties with her friends.

2. _____ Dickinson started to write poems.
   _____ Dickinson did not leave her house for 16 years.

3. _____ Dickinson became ill.
   _____ Dickinson did not let the doctor in her room.

4. _____ Dickinson's sister found her poems.
   _____ Dickinson died.

◆ TELL THE STORY

Work with a partner. Tell the story of Emily Dickinson to your partner. Use your own words. Your partner can ask you questions about the story. Then, your partner tells you the story and you ask questions.

DISCUSSION

Discuss the answers to these questions with your classmates.

1. Many great artists, musicians, or writers live alone. Why is this?

2. Why do you think Emily Dickinson wore only white?

3. Why are some people famous only after they die?

WRITING

Describe yourself and your life.

Example: *I am 21 years old. I live with my family.*

_____

_____

_____

_____

PETER ILICH
TCHAIKOVSKY
(1840–1893)

BEFORE YOU READ

Peter Ilich Tchaikovsky wrote beautiful music. What do you know about him? Are these sentences true? Check (✔) *Yes* or *No*.

1. Tchaikovsky was Polish.   ⭕ Yes   ⭕ No
2. Tchaikovsky was famous for his ballets.   ⭕ Yes   ⭕ No
3. Tchaikovsky did not hear very well.   ⭕ Yes   ⭕ No
4. Tchaikovsky was a happy person.   ⭕ Yes   ⭕ No

Now read about Peter Ilich Tchaikovsky and check your answers.

PETER ILICH TCHAIKOVSKY

Peter Ilich Tchaikovsky was born in 1840 in Russia. His family was rich and sent him to special schools. Tchaikovsky went to a university and studied law. But at the age of 23, he decided to give his life to music. He studied music in Saint Petersburg. When he was 26, he wrote his first symphony.

Tchaikovsky became a famous and successful **composer.** But he did not live a happy or exciting life. He was very shy and lived alone. Every day he stayed home and wrote music. He was often unhappy. He was afraid of many things. He was afraid to die. He was also afraid his head would fall off his shoulders. This was a problem when he **conducted** music. So he sometimes held his head with his left hand and conducted with his right hand.

In 1876, Tchaikovsky received a letter from a mysterious rich **widow.** Her name was Madame von Meck. She said she loved his music and **offered** to send him money every year. There was one **condition.** They must never meet. Tchaikovsky agreed. They wrote to each other for 14 years. Then Madame von Meck suddenly stopped writing. Tchaikovsky was very hurt. When he died three years later, he said her name.

Tchaikovsky died after he drank **contaminated** water. He was 53. Some people say he drank it by accident. Others say he drank the water to kill himself. Today we remember Tchaikovsky for his wonderful symphonies and ballets. To this day, *Swan Lake, The Sleeping Beauty,* and *The Nutcracker* are three of the world's most popular ballets.

VOCABULARY

◆ MEANING

Write the correct words in the blanks.

composer	conducted	widow
offered	condition	contaminated

1. A musician plays music. A _____ writes music.

2. Peter Ilich Tchaikovsky agreed to the _____. Then the woman sent the money.

3. Her husband died. Now she is a _____.

4. You shouldn't drink _____ water. It's dirty and can make you sick.

5. A rich woman wanted to give Tchaikovsky money. She _____ him money.

6. Tchaikovsky directed the musicians and they played his music. He _____ the musicians.

Work with a partner to answer these questions. Use complete sentences.

1. What does a *composer* do?

2. A friend comes to your house. What drink do you usually *offer?*

3. Where does a person stand when he or she *conducts* musicians?

4. In your country, do *widows* usually marry again?

5. You are going to take a new job on one *condition.* What is the condition?

COMPREHENSION

◆ UNDERSTANDING THE READING

Circle the letter of the correct answer.

1. Tchaikovsky wrote _____.
   a. symphonies   b. books   c. poems

2. Tchaikovsky was _____.
   a. a happy man   b. afraid of many things   c. not successful in his life

3. For many years Tchaikovsky _____.
   a. was sick and stayed   b. was afraid to write   c. received money
      in bed   symphonies   from a woman

◆ REMEMBERING DETAILS

Reread the passage and answer the questions.

1. Where did Tchaikovsky study music?

2. Who was the mysterious woman?

3. How long did the woman and Tchaikovsky write to each other?

4. What did the woman offer to send Tchaikovsky every year?

5. How old was Tchaikovsky when he died?

6. What is the name of one of Tchaikovsky's ballets?

◆ UNDERSTANDING THE SEQUENCE

Which happened first? Write 1 on the line. Which happened second? Write 2 on the line.

1. _____ Tchaikovsky wrote his first symphony.
   _____ Tchaikovsky became famous.

2. _____ Madame von Meck offered to send Tchaikovsky money.
   _____ Tchaikovsky received a letter.

3. _____ Tchaikovsky studied law.
   _____ Tchaikovsky studied music.

4. _____ Tchaikovsky died.
   _____ Madame von Meck stopped writing letters.

◆ TELL THE STORY

Work with a partner. Tell the story of Peter Ilich Tchaikovsky to your partner. Use your own words. Your partner can ask you questions about the story. Then, your partner tells you the story and you ask questions.

DISCUSSION

Discuss the answers to these questions with your classmates.

1. Do you know any other great composers? What are their names?

2. What kind of music do you like?

3. How would you feel if someone offered to send you money for the rest of your life?

WRITING

Write about some things you are afraid of.

Example: *I am afraid of tests. I get very nervous.*

_____

_____

_____

_____

UNIT 6
MARIE CURIE
(1867–1934)

BEFORE YOU READ

Marie Curie was one of the world's greatest scientists. What do you know about scientists and Marie Curie? Answer the questions with a partner.

1. What do scientists do?
2. What is the name of a famous scientist?
3. Do you know what made Marie Curie famous?
4. Look at the picture of Marie Curie. What do you think she is doing?

Now read about Marie Curie.

MARIE CURIE

Marie Curie was a great **scientist**. She was born Marja Sklodowska in Warsaw, Poland, in 1867. Both of her parents were teachers. When Marie was only 10 years old, her mother died.

Marie was a very good student. She loved science, math, and languages. She and her sister Bronya wanted to go to college. But in those days, only men could go to college in Poland. The girls had to go to France to study. There was not enough money for both sisters to go. So Marie worked as a teacher in Poland. She sent money to Bronya to pay for medical school in Paris. After Bronya became a doctor, she helped Marie.

When she was 24, Marie became a science student at the Sorbonne, a university in Paris. Even with her sister's help, she did not have much money. She lived in a small room near the college. It had no lights, no water, and no heat. Sometimes Marie only had bread and tea to eat.

Marie studied hard and **graduated** in 1894. A year later, she married Pierre Curie. He was also a scientist. They worked together for many years. Their most important **discovery** was radium. Today, doctors use the **rays** from radium to **treat** cancer. The Curies won a Nobel Prize for their discovery. This is the highest **award** for a scientist. Marie Curie was the first woman to receive this award.

When Marie Curie was 39, Pierre died in a road accident. But she continued their work. Curie became the first woman professor in France. In 1911, she won a second Nobel Prize. But years of working with radium **ruined** her health. She died of cancer in 1934. Her daughter Irene continued Curie's work. She also received a Nobel Prize. Sadly, Irene also got cancer and died young. Both women gave their lives for their work.

VOCABULARY

◆ MEANING

Write the correct words in the blanks.

scientist	graduated	discovery	treat
award	ruin	rays	

1. Marie Curie was a _____. She studied the world around her.

2. The sun gives out _____ of light.

3. Marie and Pierre Curie found something new. No one had found it before. Their _____ was radium.

4. Marie Curie finished her studies at the university. She _____.

5. Radium is used to_____ cancer, but too much radium can cause cancer.

6. The Nobel Prize is a prize that people receive when they do something very special. It is an important _____.

7. There are many things, like smoking, that are bad for your health. They
    _____ your health.

◆ USE

Work with a partner to answer these questions. Use complete sentences.

1. When did or when will you *graduate* from high school?

2. What is an important *discovery?* When did it happen?

3. What is the name of the *award* Marie Curie got for her work? What is another important award?

4. What are some things that can *ruin* your health?

5. What is the name of the *rays* that doctors use to take a picture of your bones?

6. What do you do to *treat* a cold?

COMPREHENSION

◆ UNDERSTANDING THE READING

Circle the letter of the correct answer.

1. Marie Curie was _____.

    a. a great scientist   b. a great doctor   c. a great scientist because
    of her husband

2. Marie Curie's work _____.

    a. made her rich   b. killed her husband   c. ruined her health

3. Today radium is used by _____.

    a. scientists to win   b. doctors to treat   c. science students to
    awards   cancer   study cancer

◆ REMEMBERING DETAILS

Reread the passage and answer the questions.

1. Where was Marie Curie born?

2. Where was the university Marie went to?

3. What was Pierre Curie's job?

4. What did the Curies discover?

5. How old was Marie Curie when her husband died?

6. When did she get a second Nobel Prize?

7. What was Curie's daughter's name?

◆ UNDERSTANDING THE SEQUENCE

Which happened first? Write 1 on the line. Which happened second? Write 2 on the line.

1. _____ Marie became a teacher in Poland.
   _____ Bronya became a doctor.

2. _____ Curie was the first woman to receive the Nobel Prize.
   _____ Curie was the first woman professor in France.

3. _____ Marie Curie became a professor in France.
   _____ Pierre Curie died in an accident.

4. _____ Curie and her husband discovered radium.
   _____ Curie and her husband won the Nobel Prize.

◆ TELL THE STORY

Work with a partner. Tell the story of Marie Curie to your partner. Use your own words. Your partner can ask you questions about the story. Then, your partner tells you the story and you ask questions.

DISCUSSION

Discuss the answers to these questions with your classmates.

1. Marie Curie gave her life for her work. In what other professions do people give their lives for their work?

2. Many diseases do not have cures. What are some of these diseases?

3. Do you think in the future there will be no disease? Why or why not?

WRITING

Write about a job you like.

Example: *Teaching is a good job. A teacher has a lot of vacation.*

_____

_____

_____

_____

UNIT 7

MADAM C. J. WALKER
(1867–1919)

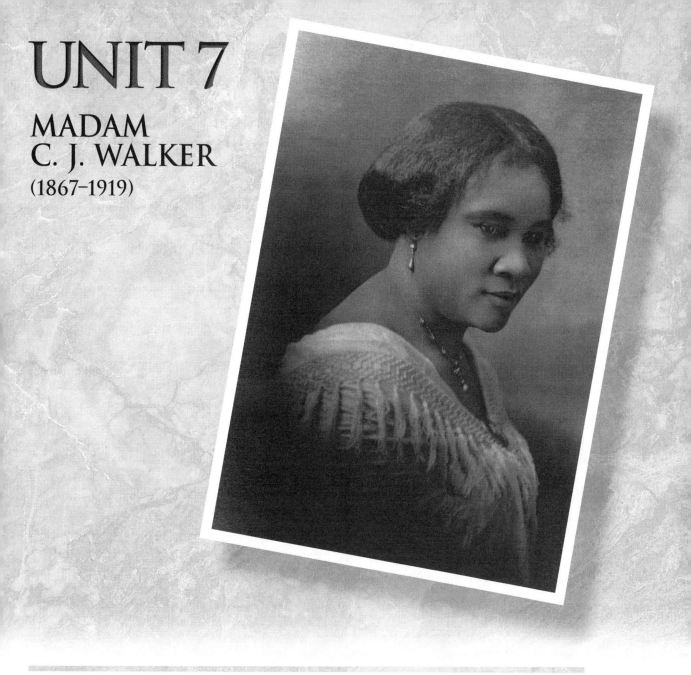

BEFORE YOU READ

Madam C. J. Walker started her own company for hair care and beauty products. What do you know about beauty products? Answer the questions with a partner.

1. L'Oréal™ is one famous brand name in beauty products. What are some other famous brand names in beauty products?
2. Why do people use brand name products?
3. Look at the picture of Madam C. J. Walker. What can you say about her?

Now read about Madam C. J. Walker.

MADAM C. J. WALKER

Madam C. J. Walker was the first African American woman in the United States to make a million dollars. She was born Sarah Breedlove in 1867 on a farm in Delta, Louisiana. Her family was very poor, and her life was very hard. They lived in a small house with a **dirt** floor and no windows. Sarah did not go to school. Every day she worked from morning to night in the cotton **fields.**

When Sarah was seven, her parents died. She went to Mississippi to live with her married sister. Her sister's husband was very mean to her. Sarah wanted to get away, so she got married when she was 14. A few years later, she had a baby girl named Lelia. When Sarah was only 20, her husband died. She moved to St. Louis, Missouri. For the next 18 years, she worked washing clothes for $1.50 a day. When she was 38, Sarah was worried because her hair was falling out. She tried different things on her hair, but nothing worked. One night she had a dream about what to mix up and use for her hair. It worked! Sarah gave it to her friends. It worked for them, too. She went from door to door to sell her new hair **product.** Then she made other hair care products. Soon she had her own business.

Sarah Breedlove married Charles Joseph Walker and opened several beauty shops under the name of Madam C. J. Walker. In 1910, she built a factory to make hair care products and face creams. By 1917, her company was the most successful African American–owned business in the United States. She started her business with only $1.50, but now she was rich. She had a **mansion** in New York. Madam Walker also gave a lot of money to **charity.** She wanted to help African Americans, especially women. But she did not enjoy her good life for very long. Madam Walker died at the age of 52. She left two-thirds of her **fortune** to charity. Her **will** said that the head of the C. J. Walker Company must always be a woman.

VOCABULARY

◆ MEANING

Write the correct words in the blanks.

fields	product	mansion	dirt
charity	will	fortune	

1. Sarah Breedlove's house did not have a wood or stone floor. The floor was just _____.

2. On a farm, the horses and cows stay outside in the _____.

3. Walker made a lot of money from her discovery. She made a _____.

4. Shampoo is one kind of hair care _____.

5. Walker loved to help the poor. She gave a lot of money to _____.

6. Walker had a _____ in New York. It was a big, beautiful, expensive house.

7. Walker decided what to do with her money. Before she died, she wrote it down on a piece of paper. She wrote a _____.

◆ USE

Work with a partner to answer these questions. Use complete sentences.

1. What grows in *fields?*
2. Do you use any *products* on your hair? What are they?
3. What is an easy way to make a *fortune?*
4. What do people write in a *will?*
5. What *charities* do people give money to?

COMPREHENSION

◆ UNDERSTANDING THE READING

Circle the letter of the correct answer.

1. When she was young, Walker had _____.
   a. problems with her hair   b. a small business   c. a hard life

2. Walker started her business by making a product for _____.
   a. her sister   b. Lelia   c. herself

3. Walker was the first African American woman to _____.
   a. start a business   b. make a million dollars   c. use another name

◆ REMEMBERING DETAILS

Circle T if the sentence is true. Circle F if it is false.

	True	False
1. After age seven, Sarah lived with her mother.	T	F
2. At age 38, Walker's hair started to fall out.	T	F
3. Walker married two times.	T	F
4. In 1910, her husband built a factory.	T	F
5. She left her fortune to her daughter.	T	F
6. The head of Walker's company must always be a woman.	T	F

◆ UNDERSTANDING THE SEQUENCE

Which happened first? Write 1 on the line. Which happened second? Write 2 on the line.

1. _____ Sarah worked washing clothes.
   _____ Sarah worked in the fields.

2. _____ Sarah had a dream about her hair.
   _____ Sarah's hair was falling out.

3. _____ Sarah married C. J. Walker.
   _____ Sarah opened beauty shops.

4. _____ Walker built a factory.
   _____ Walker went from door to door selling her products.

◆ TELL THE STORY

Work with a partner. Tell the story of Madam C. J. Walker to your partner. Use your own words. Your partner can ask you questions about the story. Then, your partner tells you the story and you ask questions.

DISCUSSION

Discuss the answers to these questions with your classmates.

1. If you had a chance to start a company, what kind of company would it be? Why?

2. Did you ever have a dream that came true?

3. How would you change your hair?

WRITING

Write about where you lived when you were a child.

Example: *I lived in a small town. We had a small house.*

_____

_____

_____

_____

UNIT 8

ALBERT EINSTEIN
(1879–1955)

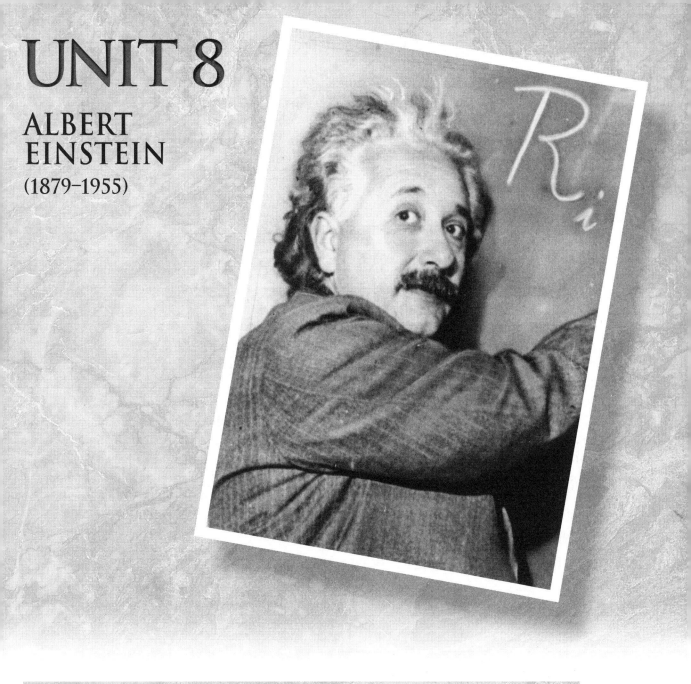

BEFORE YOU READ

Albert Einstein was one of the world's greatest scientists. What do you know about him? Are these sentences true? Check (✔) *Yes* or *No*.

1. Einstein was born in Germany.   ○ Yes ○ No
2. Einstein was a good student when he was young.   ○ Yes ○ No
3. Einstein often forgot things.   ○ Yes ○ No
4. Einstein was a teacher.   ○ Yes ○ No

Now read about Albert Einstein and check your answers.

ALBERT EINSTEIN

Albert Einstein is one of the greatest scientists who ever lived. But he couldn't find his way home when he went for a walk. He dressed in **wrinkled** clothes and an old coat. He often forgot things. Once he used a $1,500 check to **mark** a page in a book. Then he lost the book! Einstein had other things to think about. Science was more important to him than the **ordinary** things in life.

Albert Einstein was born in 1879 in Ulm, Germany. When he was a child, he learned things very slowly. Albert didn't speak until he was three years old. His parents worried about him. The **principal** of his school told his father, "Your son will never make a success of anything." His grades in school were bad. The only thing he liked to do was play the violin.

When he was 12, Albert began reading math and science books. He was excited about the things he learned. At age 17, he started college in Switzerland. Einstein wanted to be a teacher. He graduated in 1900, but he could not find a job. A friend helped him get a job in a government office.

While he was in school, Einstein became more and more interested in math and **physics.** He wanted to find the answers to questions about the **universe.** In 1905, Einstein published his ideas. At first, other scientists laughed at them. But Einstein's **theory** of relativity changed the world. Scientists looked at the universe in a new way. Because of Einstein, we have such things as computers, television, and space travel today.

Einstein quickly became famous. He traveled around the world and talked about his ideas. In 1922, he received the Nobel Prize for physics. In 1933, Adolf Hitler came to power in Germany. Life became difficult for Jews like Einstein. So Einstein moved to America. He lived and taught in Princeton, New Jersey, for 22 years until he died in 1955. He once said, "The important thing is not to stop questioning." Albert Einstein never did.

VOCABULARY

◆ MEANING

Write the correct words in the blanks.

mark	ordinary	principal	universe
wrinkled	theory	physics	

1. When clothes get _____, we iron them.

2. Albert Einstein was not _____. He was a genius.

3. The speed of light is one thing you study in _____.

4. The head of a school is called a _____.

5. Einstein used a $1,500 check to _____ a page in a book.

6. The stars, the planets, and space together are the _____.

7. A _____ is an idea that explains something.

◆ USE

Work with a partner to answer these questions. Use complete sentences.

1. What do you use to *mark* a page in a book?

2. What does a high school *principal* do?

3. Do you know someone who is not *ordinary?*

4. Do you want to travel across the *universe?* Why or why not?

5. What things get *wrinkled?*

6. Do you like *physics?* Why or why not?

COMPREHENSION

◆ UNDERSTANDING THE READING

Circle the letter of the correct answer.

1. As a child, Einstein didn't _____.
   a. learn quickly   b. work hard   c. play the violin

2. Einstein became famous because of his ideas about _____.
   a. scientists   b. the Nobel Prize   c. the universe

3. From Einstein's story, we learn that it is important to _____.
   a. study hard   b. question everything   c. remember everything

◆ REMEMBERING DETAILS

Reread the passage and answer the questions.

1. What did Einstein use to mark a page?

2. In which country was Einstein born?

3. Why did Einstein's parents worry?

4. At what age did Einstein begin reading math and science books?

5. When did Einstein get the Nobel Prize?

6. Where did Einstein die?

Which happened first? Write 1 on the line. Which happened second? Write 2 on the line.

1. _____ Einstein began reading math and science books.
   _____ Einstein was a poor student.

2. _____ Einstein published his ideas.
   _____ Einstein became famous.

3. _____ Einstein left Germany.
   _____ Einstein got the Nobel Prize.

4. _____ Einstein traveled around the world.
   _____ Einstein worked at Princeton University.

◆ TELL THE STORY

Work with a partner. Tell the story of Albert Einstein to your partner. Use your own words. Your partner can ask you questions about the story. Then, your partner tells you the story and you ask questions.

DISCUSSION

Discuss the answers to these questions with your classmates.

1. What is your favorite subject? Do you like to study science?

2. Einstein was very intelligent, but he forgot many simple things. Why is this? Do you know other people like Einstein? Describe them.

3. Do you think countries should spend a lot of money on space travel?

WRITING

Describe what you think the world will be like 200 years from now.

Example: *We will have vacations on the moon.*

_____

_____

_____

_____

UNIT 9
PABLO PICASSO
(1881–1973)

BEFORE YOU READ

Pablo Picasso was one of the world's most famous artists. What do you know about him? Are these sentences true? Check (✔) *Yes* or *No*.

1. Picasso was Italian.   ○ Yes   ○ No
2. Picasso was very famous in his lifetime.   ○ Yes   ○ No
3. Picasso had a short life.   ○ Yes   ○ No
4. Picasso was a strange man.   ○ Yes   ○ No

Now read about Pablo Picasso and check your answers.

PABLO PICASSO

Pablo Picasso **drew** pictures before he could talk. As a child, he sat happily with his paper and pencils and drew for hours. His father was a painter. He was very happy that his son liked to draw, but he did not know that one day Pablo would be one of the greatest artists of the twentieth **century.**

Pablo Picasso was born in 1881 in Malaga, Spain. He was a very bad student, and he hated school. Instead of studying, he drew pictures. When he was only eight years old, he finished his first oil painting. It had beautiful colors. Picasso never sold this painting.

When Pablo was 14, his family moved to Barcelona. He wanted to go to the School of Fine Arts. To get into the school, a student had to finish a painting in one month. Picasso finished his painting in one day.

When he was 18, Picasso went to live in Paris. He was very poor at first. He lived in a small room and worked with only the light of a **candle.** Sometimes he did not even have money for a candle. But Pablo Picasso had a strong personality. He believed in himself. He **created** one piece of art after another. He met important people, and they began to buy his work. **Eventually** Picasso became rich and famous.

Picasso was strange in many ways. For example, for a long time, he did not want a telephone. Then one day his son almost died because he could not call for help. Picasso was also strange because he did not throw anything away, not even an empty cigarette package. He liked to be alone, so he **locked** his **studio.** No one could get in. Picasso loved animals. He had a monkey, a goat, snakes, and many dogs. He was married twice, and he was not very close to his family and friends. His work was more important to him than people were.

Picasso lived a long and full life. He never stopped working. He painted 200 pictures the year he was 90. He was still working on the day he died at the age of 91. Picasso left the world the genius of his art.

VOCABULARY

◆ MEANING

Write the correct words in the blanks.

drew	candle	created	century
eventually	lock	studio	

1. You should _____ your door at night. It's important to be safe.

2. At first Pablo Picasso was not famous. After a lot of work, he _____ became famous.

3. Picasso was born in 1881, during the nineteenth _____.

4. An artist works in a _____.

5. Young Picasso was poor. He didn't have a lamp. He had to work by the light of a _____.

6. Picasso worked hard and _____ many paintings. He finished more than 200 paintings the year he was 90.

7. Picasso used paper and pencil and _____ pictures instead of studying.

◆ USE

Work with a partner to answer these questions. Use complete sentences.

1. *Draw* a picture for your partner. What did you draw? Describe it.

2. When do people use *candles?*

3. Picasso *created* paintings. What other things do artists create?

4. You are studying English. *Eventually* what will you be able to do?

5. What is something that you always *lock?*

6. What do you think will happen in the twenty-first *century?*

COMPREHENSION

◆ UNDERSTANDING THE READING

Circle the letter of the correct answer.

1. Picasso created many _____.
   a. stories   b. studios   c. paintings

2. Picasso always _____.
   a. moved   b. worked   c. lived alone

3. Picasso was famous _____.
   a. when he was young   b. during his lifetime   c. because of one painting

◆ REMEMBERING DETAILS

Reread the passage and answer the questions.

1. What was Picasso's father's profession?

2. What country was Picasso from?

3. How old was Picasso when he finished his first painting?

4. Where did Picasso go when he was 18?

5. How many paintings did he make when he was 90?

6. How old was Picasso when he died?

◆ UNDERSTANDING THE SEQUENCE

Which happened first? Write 1 on the line. Which happened second? Write 2 on the line.

1. _____ Picasso talked.
   _____ Picasso drew pictures.

2. _____ Picasso finished his first painting.
   _____ Picasso went to the School of Fine Arts.

3. _____ Picasso became famous.
   _____ Picasso moved to Paris.

4. _____ Picasso bought a telephone.
   _____ Picasso's son almost died.

◆ TELL THE STORY

Work with a partner. Tell the story of Pablo Picasso to your partner. Use your own words. Your partner can ask you questions about the story. Then, your partner tells you the story and you ask questions.

DISCUSSION

Discuss the answers to these questions with your classmates.

1. Did you ever see a painting by Picasso? What did it look like?
2. Picasso liked to be alone. Do you like to be alone? Do you know anyone who does? Describe them.
3. Do you like art museums? Why or why not?

WRITING

Describe the life of an older person you know.

Example: *My grandfather is 85. He lives with us.*

_____

_____

_____

_____

UNIT 10

JEAN PAUL GETTY

(1892–1976)

BEFORE YOU READ

At one time, Jean Paul Getty was the richest man in the world. What do you know about rich people? Answer the questions with a partner.

1. Who are some of the richest people in the world today?
2. What do they do with their money?
3. How did these people become so rich?
4. Look at the picture of Jean Paul Getty. What can you say about him?

Now read about Jean Paul Getty.

JEAN PAUL GETTY

Jean Paul Getty was born in 1892 in Minneapolis, Minnesota. He became a millionaire when he was only 24. His father was **wealthy,** but he did not help his son. Getty made his millions alone. Like his father, he made his money from oil. He owned Getty Oil and over 100 other companies. One magazine called Getty "the richest man in the world."

But money did not buy happiness for Getty. He married five times and divorced five times. He had five children but spent little time with them. None of Getty's children had very happy lives.

Getty cared a lot about money. He loved to make money and loved to save it. He was a very **stingy** man. Every evening, he wrote down every cent he spent that day. He lived in England in a house with 72 bedrooms. He put pay telephones in his guests' bedrooms so he could save money on phone bills.

In 1973, **kidnappers** took his grandson. They asked for money to **release** the boy. Getty's son asked his father for money to save his child. Getty **refused.** So the kidnappers cut off the boy's ear. Finally, Getty **lent** the money to his son, but at 4 percent **interest.**

Getty had another side. He loved to collect art. He started a museum at his home in Malibu, California. He bought many important and beautiful pieces of art for the museum. When Getty died in 1976, the value of the art in the museum was $1 billion. He left all his money to the museum. After his death, the museum grew in size. Today it is one of the most important museums in the United States. Getty made his money from oil. But he gave his money to the art world because he wanted people to learn about and love art.

VOCABULARY

◆ MEANING

Write the correct words in the blanks.

wealthy	stingy	release	refused
kidnappers	lent	interest	

1. When you give someone $100 at 4 percent _____, they will pay you back $104.

2. _____ took Getty's grandson. They said they wanted money or they would hurt the boy.

3. Getty became very _____, just like his father. They both made millions of dollars.

4. When you _____ something, you let it go.

5. Getty loved money more than people. He _____ to give the kidnappers any money.

6. Getty didn't like to give money away. However, he _____ money to his son.

7. Getty did not like to share. He was a _____ man.

◆ USE

Work with a partner to answer these questions. Use complete sentences.

1. Do you know any *wealthy* people? How did they become wealthy?

2. What does a *stingy* person do?

3. How much is 6 percent *interest* on $100?

4. What does a *kidnapper* do? Why?

5. What is something that you *refuse* to do?

6. Do you ever *lend* money to your friends? Why or why not?

COMPREHENSION

◆ UNDERSTANDING THE READING

Circle the letter of the correct answer.

1. Getty wasn't _____.
   a. stingy   b. happy   c. rich

2. Getty's children were _____.
   a. stingy   b. unhappy   c. poor

3. Besides money, Getty also liked _____.
   a. art   b. children   c. work

◆ REMEMBERING DETAILS

Reread the passage and answer the questions.

1. What did Jean Paul Getty make his money from?

2. How many times did he get married?

3. Where was his house with 72 bedrooms?

4. Who did the kidnappers take?

5. What did Getty's son ask from his father?

6. Where did Getty build a museum?

7. When did he die?

Which happened first? Write 1 on the line. Which happened second? Write 2 on the line.

1. _____ Getty was called "the richest man in the world."
   _____ Getty made millions of dollars alone.

2. _____ Kidnappers took Getty's grandson.
   _____ Kidnappers asked for money to release the boy.

3. _____ Getty gave money to his son.
   _____ The kidnappers cut off the boy's ear.

4. _____ Getty built an art museum.
   _____ Getty left all his money to an art museum.

◆ TELL THE STORY

Work with a partner. Tell the story of Jean Paul Getty to your partner. Use your own words. Your partner can ask you questions about the story. Then, your partner tells you the story and you ask questions.

DISCUSSION

Discuss the answers to these questions with your classmates.

1. What do you think about Jean Paul Getty?

2. Can money buy happiness? Why or why not?

3. Do you know about any kidnappers? What do you know about them?

WRITING

Imagine you are very rich. Describe what your life is like.

Example: *I live on an island. I have my own airplane.*

_____

_____

_____

_____

UNIT 11

OSEOLA McCARTY
(1909–1999)

BEFORE YOU READ

Oseola McCarty worked hard and saved all her money. When she was 86, she began to give money to others. Imagine you are 86 years old. You have $250,000. You have no children. What would you do with the money? Discuss your answers with a partner.

- Give it to poor or sick people.
- Spend it on yourself.
- Spend it on other members of your family.
- Give it to a school.
- Keep it in a bank.
- Other: _____

Now read about Oseola McCarty.

OSEOLA McCARTY

In 1995, Oseola McCarty gave a **gift** of $150,000 to the University of Southern Mississippi. She wanted to help poor students. It was a very **generous** thing to do. But her friends and neighbors were surprised. McCarty was a good woman. She went to church. She was always friendly and helpful. But everyone in her town knew that McCarty was not rich. In fact, she was poor.

How did a poor 86-year-old woman have so much money? Oseola McCarty was born in 1908 in Hattiesburg, Mississippi. She had to leave school when she was eight years old to help her family. She took a job washing clothes. She **earned** only a few dollars a day. Oseola washed the clothes by hand. Then she hung the clothes to dry. She did this for nearly 80 years. In the 1960s, she bought an automatic washer and dryer. But she gave them away. She did not think they got the clothes clean enough! At that time, many people started to buy their own washers and dryers. McCarty did not have much work, so she started to iron clothes instead.

McCarty never married or had children. Her life was very simple. She went to work and to church. She read her Bible. She had a black-and-white television. But she did not watch it very much. It had only one channel.

McCarty saved money all her life and eventually had about $250,000. When she was 86, a lawyer helped her make a will. She left money to the church, her **relatives,** and the university. McCarty just wanted to help others. She did not think she was a special person. But then people **found out** about her gift to the university. She received many **honors.** She even flew in an airplane for the first time!

Oseola McCarty died in 1999. She was a shy and **humble** woman who became famous.

VOCABULARY

◆ MEANING

Write the correct words in the blanks.

gift	earned	generous	relatives
found out	humble	honors	

1. Oseola McCarty _____ money by washing clothes.
2. Your grandparents, aunts, uncles, and cousins are your _____.
3. McCarty didn't think she was special. She was a _____ person.
4. People showed McCarty respect in public. They gave her many _____.
5. McCarty gave a present to the University of Southern Mississippi. Everyone was surprised by the _____ of $150,000.

6. People did not know McCarty left her money to the school. Then they heard about it. They _____ about it.

7. A _____ person likes to give to others.

◆ USE

Work with a partner to answer these questions. Use complete sentences.

1. What is the best *gift* a person can give?

2. In what jobs can you *earn* a good salary?

3. What is something *generous* that you did?

4. How many *relatives* do you have?

5. How do you *find out* someone's telephone number without asking him or her?

6. What do people do to receive *honors?*

COMPREHENSION

◆ UNDERSTANDING THE READING

Circle the letter of the correct answer.

1. Oseola McCarty _____.

   a. earned a lot of money every day   b. had many expensive things   c. earned money by washing clothes

2. McCarty gave most of her money to _____.

   a. her relatives   b. the university   c. her church

3. Everyone was surprised because they thought McCarty had no _____.

   a. money   b. education   c. relatives

◆ REMEMBERING DETAILS

Circle T if the sentence is true. Circle F if it is false.

	True	False
1. McCarty left school in the eighth grade.	T	F
2. She washed clothes by hand.	T	F
3. She watched television a lot.	T	F
4. McCarty gave $250,000 to the University of Southern Mississippi.	T	F
5. She left no money to the church.	T	F
6. She made a will.	T	F

◆ SENTENCE COMPLETION

Match the words in Column A and Column B to make sentences.

A	B
___ 1. McCarty's life was	a. to the university.
___ 2. She went	b. clothes.
___ 3. She had	c. a hardworking woman.
___ 4. She was	d. simple.
___ 5. She left money	e. a black-and-white television.
___ 6. She washed	f. to work and to church.

◆ DICTATION

Work with a partner. Read four sentences from the exercise above. Your partner listens and writes the sentences. Then, your partner reads four sentences and you write them.

DISCUSSION

Discuss the answers to these questions with your classmates.

1. Is it good to save money or spend it?

2. Did you ever do something that surprised other people? What?

3. What do you think the University of Southern Mississippi did with McCarty's gift?

WRITING

Write about what you do to help other people.

Example: *Every week I buy bread for my neighbor.*

_____

_____

_____

_____

UNIT 12

BABE DIDRIKSON ZAHARIAS

(1911–1956)

BEFORE YOU READ

Babe Didrikson Zaharias was one of the most famous athletes of the twentieth century. What do you know about athletes? Answer the questions with a partner.

1. Who are some famous athletes?
2. How does a person become a sports star?
3. Can one person be "number one" in several sports?
4. Look at the picture of Babe Didrikson Zaharias. What do you think she is doing?

Now read about Babe Didrikson Zaharias.

BABE DIDRIKSON ZAHARIAS

Babe Didrikson Zaharias was one of the greatest American **athletes** of modern times. She was born Mildred Didrikson in 1911 in Port Arthur, Texas. As a child, she played baseball, basketball, and tennis. She also enjoyed running and other sports. Mildred was great at all of them. One day she hit five home runs in a baseball game. Then everyone called her "Babe" after the famous baseball player Babe Ruth.

Zaharias had many interests. She was very **talented.** She played musical instruments. She sewed clothes very well, and she won first prize at a state fair. She became an excellent ballroom dancer and a great **chef.** But she liked sports best.

In 1932, Zaharias tried out for the Olympic games. She won four **events** in three hours. Her **performance** was the greatest in the history of athletics. During the games, she won two gold medals and one silver medal.

Everyone said that Zaharias was a great athlete. But they also said bad things about her because she was a woman. In those days, many women did not work. People believed that women should stay at home. Zaharias was lonely and hurt sometimes. Then she married professional wrestler George Zaharias. He left his job to be Zaharias's manager. People said things about that, too!

Zaharias decided to **concentrate** on golf. She practiced 16 hours a day. Sometimes her hands were bloody from practicing. She became a champion. She won 82 **tournaments.**

Sadly, Babe Didrikson Zaharias died at a young age. She was 45. She was the only female sports hero of her time. She was an important role model for female athletes in the United States.

VOCABULARY

◆ MEANING

Write the correct words in the blanks.

athletes	talented	chef	performance
concentrate	tournament	events	

1. The World Cup is the most important _____ in the game of soccer.

2. There are many different games in the Olympics. Babe Didrikson Zaharias won four _____ in three hours.

3. Zaharias had a great _____ in the 1932 Olympics. She won gold and silver medals.

4. After the Olympics, Zaharias wanted to give special attention to just one sport. She decided to _____ on golf.

5. People who play sports are called _____.

6. Zaharias had a natural ability to do things. She was _____.

7. Zaharias was a wonderful cook. She was a great _____.

◆ USE

Work with a partner to answer these questions. Use complete sentences.

1. Who is someone you know that is very *talented?*

2. What does a *chef* do?

3. What is your favorite *event* in the Olympics?

4. What movie star gives the best *performance?*

5. When do you *concentrate* a lot?

6. Who is your favorite *athlete?*

COMPREHENSION

◆ UNDERSTANDING THE READING

Circle the letter of the correct answer.

1. People remember Zaharias as a great _____.
   a. athlete   b. chef   c. dancer

2. People said bad things about Zaharias because she didn't _____.
   a. win gold medals   b. marry George Zaharias   c. act like a woman

3. Zaharias opened the way for _____ athletes.
   a. young   b. female   c. African American

◆ REMEMBERING DETAILS

Reread the passage and answer the questions.

1. How many home runs did Mildred hit in one day?

2. What famous baseball player was Mildred named after?

3. How many gold medals did she win at the Olympics?

4. Who did she marry?

5. What sport did she practice after she got married?

6. How many tournaments did she win?

Match the words in Column A and Column B to make sentences.

A	B
___ 1. She married	a. a great chef.
___ 2. She played	b. three Olympic medals.
___ 3. She was	c. clothes.
___ 4. She sewed	d. musical instruments.
___ 5. She won	e. left his job.
___ 6. Her husband	f. a wrestler.

◆ DICTATION

Work with a partner. Read four sentences from the exercise above. Your partner listens and writes the sentences. Then, your partner reads four sentences and you write them.

DISCUSSION

Discuss the answers to these questions with your classmates.

1. Why do you think Zaharias is called a "sports hero"?

2. Zaharias was talented at many things. What are you talented at?

3. Do men and women play the same sports? What is a sport played only by men? *footba*
   What is one played only by women?

WRITING

Write about a sports star or someone who plays sports.

Example: *My favorite sports person is my brother. He plays soccer very well.*

_____

_____

_____

_____

UNIT 13
MINORU YAMASAKI
(1912–1986)

BEFORE YOU READ

Minoru Yamasaki was an architect. He designed many famous buildings. What do you know about famous buildings? Answer the questions with a partner.

1. What are three famous buildings around the world?
2. Which of these buildings is the biggest?
3. Are all famous buildings very big?
4. Look at the picture of Minoru Yamasaki. What can you say about him?

Now read about Minoru Yamasaki.

MINORU YAMASAKI

Minoru Yamasaki was a well-known American architect. He was born in 1912 in Seattle, Washington. His parents came from Japan. Minoru went to college to study architecture. Every summer he worked in a fish factory to help pay for college. Often he worked from four o'clock in the morning until midnight. He slept in a room with 100 other men. Later in life, Yamasaki remembered these times and was always good to his workers.

Yamasaki sometimes dreamed about his work. Once he woke up at three o'clock in the morning. He remembered a building that was in his dream. He got up and started to draw. Yamasaki used a new **design** for the buildings. These buildings are now the Century Plaza Hotel and Tower in Los Angeles, California.

Yamasaki was different from other architects. His buildings give people a feeling of **peace** and happiness. Many of his designs have **pools** of water, flowers, and windows on the **roof** to let in light.

He always designed buildings to **please** people. He wanted to give them a place away from the busy ways of modern life.

Yamasaki worked for several companies. But his success began when he started his own company. In 1956, he won the Architect's First Honor Award for his design of an airport in St. Louis, Missouri. He won two more awards over the next five years. In 1962, he designed the World Trade Center in New York. It is very famous.

In 1993, a bomb exploded in the World Trade Center. But the buildings did not fall down because they had a good design. Sadly, in 2001 two planes crashed into the World Trade Center and the buildings fell.

Yamasaki had strong **opinions** about his buildings. They had to be built his way. He refused to change the design of his buildings, even if he lost a job.

Minoru Yamasaki died in 1986. He designed more than 300 buildings. People will enjoy the design and beauty of his buildings for a very long time.

VOCABULARY

◆ MEANING

What is the meaning of the underlined words? Circle the letter of the best answer.

1. Minoru Yamasaki used a new <u>design</u> for the buildings.

    a. plan   b. height

2. His buildings give people a feeling of <u>peace</u>.

    a. home   b. quiet

3. Many of his designs have <u>pools</u> of water.

    a. fountains   b. small areas

4. They have windows on the <u>roof</u>.

    a. top of the building   b. the entrance

5. Yamasaki always designed buildings to <u>please</u> people.

   a. make people think   b. make people happy

6. Yamasaki had strong <u>opinions</u> about his buildings.

   a. beliefs   b. hopes

◆ USE

Work with a partner to answer these questions. Use complete sentences.

1. What are some things that have a nice *design?*

2. What do you have strong *opinions* about?

3. On which day of the week do you feel *peace?*

4. What do you do to *please* your teacher?

COMPREHENSION

◆ UNDERSTANDING THE READING

Circle the letter of the correct answer.

1. In Minoru Yamasaki's buildings, people feel _____.

   a. modern life   b. peace and happiness   c. noise

2. Yamasaki's buildings are famous for their _____.

   a. design   b. dreams   c. pools

3. Yamasaki had a dream about _____.

   a. starting a company   b. the World Trade Center   c. a building

◆ REMEMBERING DETAILS

Circle T if the sentence is true. Circle F if it is false.

	True	False
1. Yamasaki was born in Japan.	T	F
2. Yamasaki designed the World Trade Center.	T	F
3. Yamasaki was always nice to his workers.	T	F
4. Yamasaki won two awards in his life.	T	F
5. Yamasaki designed 200 buildings.	T	F

◆ UNDERSTANDING THE SEQUENCE

Which happened first? Write 1 on the line. Which happened second? Write 2 on the line.

1. _____ Yamasaki worked in a fish factory.
   _____ Yamasaki went to college.

2. _____ Yamasaki started his own company.
   _____ Yamasaki worked for several companies.

3. _____ Yamasaki had a dream.
   _____ Yamasaki started drawing a building.

4. _____ Yamasaki won an award for the design of an airport.
   _____ Yamasaki designed the World Trade Center.

◆ TELL THE STORY

Work with a partner. Tell the story of Minoru Yamasaki to your partner. Use your own words. Your partner can ask you questions about the story. Then, your partner tells you the story and you ask questions.

DISCUSSION

Discuss the answers to these questions with your classmates.

1. How can dreams change our lives? Give examples from your own life or other people you know.

2. What does your dream house look like?

3. Do you like modern buildings? Why or why not?

WRITING

Describe your room, apartment, or house. Do you like it? Why or why not?

Example: *My room is on the second floor. It is quiet. I have one window.*

_____

_____

_____

_____

UNIT 14

AKIO MORITA
(1921–1999)

BEFORE YOU READ

Akio Morita started the Sony company. The brand name Sony is famous around the world. What do you know about brand names? Answer the questions with a partner.

1. Why do people look for a brand name?
2. What are some famous brand names for electronic products?
3. What brands do you use? Why?
4. Look at the picture of Akio Morita. What can you say about him?

Now read about Akio Morita.

AKIO MORITA

Akio Morita was born in 1921 in Nagoya, Japan. For 14 **generations,** his family owned a company that made a rice drink called *sake*. His family wanted him to work in their business. But Akio wanted to have his own business. He and his **partner,** Masaru Ibuka, started the Sony company. It is one of the most successful companies in the world.

Morita had some ideas that were new to business. They were not **typical.** First, he wanted people to think of **quality** when they heard the name Sony. Second, he wanted to make and sell his products around the world. Morita and his partner created many new products. In 1957, Sony produced a very small radio. It was so small that it fit in a pocket. Next, they made an eight-inch television and a videotape recorder. Years later, Morita decided to create a small tape recorder. It was **portable.** People could carry it with them and listen to music. The tape recorder also had headphones. He called it the Walkman. All of these products were very popular. They were also very good. After a while, people started to buy Sony products because of the high quality. Morita's idea worked!

In 1963, Morita and his family moved to the United States. He wanted to understand the American way of life. Then he could make products that Americans liked. His plans worked again. Sony became the most popular **brand** in the United States.

Morita was a **brilliant** businessman. People started to call him "Mr. Sony". He traveled around the world and met world leaders and businesspeople. He worked very hard. He also enjoyed other activities. He went to plays and concerts. He gave big parties and attended important events. He loved to play sports. Even in his sixties, he learned new sports. He liked to water ski and play tennis. Akio Morita lived a very full life. He died at the age of 78. He worked hard, and he saw many of his dreams come true.

VOCABULARY

◆ MEANING

Write the correct words in the blanks.

generations	typical	partner	portable
brand	brilliant	quality	

1. Names like Sony, Johnson & Johnson, and Gucci are _____ names.

2. Akio Morita was a genius as a businessman. He was _____.

3. Morita had different ideas. He was not a_____ businessman.

4. Morita's family owned a company that made *sake* for many years. The company had made *sake* for 14 _____.

5. Morita and Ibuka both owned the company. Ibuka was Morita's _____.

6. Morita wanted Sony products to be good. He cared about the _____ of the products.

7. Something that is small and easy to carry with you is _____.

◆ USE

Work with a partner to answer these questions. Use complete sentences.

1. How many *generations* of your family do you know?

2. What is an example of a product of good *quality?*

3. What is a *typical* activity in your day?

4. What is something *portable?*

5. What is your favorite *brand* of candy?

6. Who is a *brilliant* person? Why is he or she brilliant?

COMPREHENSION

◆ UNDERSTANDING THE READING

Circle the letter of the correct answer.

1. Sony products are famous for their _____.
   a. quality   b. price   c. size

2. Morita always lived _____.
   a. with his partner   b. a very active life   c. in the United States

3. Morita wanted to _____ around the world and he did it.
   a. sell his products   b. travel with Ibuka   c. move his family

◆ REMEMBERING DETAILS

Reread the passage and answer the questions.

1. Where was Akio Morita born?

2. What did the Morita family business make?

3. What did Sony produce in 1957?

4. What did Morita call the small tape recorder people can carry around with them?

5. Why did people start buying Sony products?

6. When did Morita move his family to the United States?

7. What name did people call Morita?

◆ UNDERSTANDING THE SEQUENCE

Which happened first? Write 1 on the line. Which happened second? Write 2 on the line.

1. _____ Morita wanted his own business.
   _____ Ibuka and Morita started their company, Sony.

2. _____ Sony produced a pocket radio.
   _____ Sony made an eight-inch television.

3. _____ Sony produced the Walkman.
   _____ Morita had an idea for a portable tape recorder.

4. _____ Sony became the number one brand in the United States.
   _____ Morita moved his family to the United States.

◆ TELL THE STORY

Work with a partner. Tell the story of Akio Morita to your partner. Use your own words. Your partner can ask you questions about the story. Then, your partner tells you the story and you ask questions.

DISCUSSION

Discuss the answers to these questions with your classmates.

1. Morita worked all the time. He never stopped doing things. What do you think of his lifestyle?

2. What makes you buy a certain product? Is it the price, quality, brand name, or something else?

3. Name some countries and the products or brand names they are famous for.

WRITING

Describe your favorite electronic product. Explain why you like it.

Example: *My favorite electronic product is my answering machine.*

_____

_____

_____

_____

UNIT 15
MARIA CALLAS
(1923–1977)

Before you read

Maria Callas was a famous opera singer. What do you know about opera? Answer the questions with a partner.

1. Have you ever seen an opera? Which one?
2. What happens in an opera?
3. Do you know the names of any opera singers?
4. Look at the picture of Maria Callas. What do you think she is doing?

Now read about Maria Callas.

MARIA CALLAS

Maria Callas was born Maria Anna Sofia Cecilia Kalogeropoulus in New York City in 1923. Her parents were from Greece. Her mother wanted her children to study music. When Maria was seven and her sister was 13, they began singing and piano lessons.

Maria had a beautiful voice but she was very shy. Her mother **forced** her daughter to sing at **contests** and on radio programs. Maria won many top prizes, but she wasn't very happy.

Maria's father did not want to pay for expensive music lessons. He and his wife **argued.** When Maria was 13, she moved to Greece with her mother and sister. Her mother **lied** about Maria's age and got her into the Athens Conservatory. Maria studied hard for two years. She had no time for friends or fun.

In 1939, Maria began to study with a world-famous Spanish opera singer, Elvira de Hidalgo. She changed Maria's life. De Hidalgo taught her to sing and act. She also taught her how to fix her hair and choose beautiful clothes. Maria joined Greece's National Opera at age 16 and took the stage name Maria Callas. At 17, she was a **permanent** member. She was the youngest person ever to join a European opera company.

Soon Callas became an international star. Some called her the "Golden Voice of the Century." She acted and sang with great **emotion.** Her style changed opera forever. In 1947, she joined La Scala, the leading opera house in Milan. By age 24, Callas was giving 50 performances a year. Some people said this was not good for her singing voice.

Sadly, Callas was not happy. She argued with everyone and did not get along with other singers. She had a problem with her **throat** and started to lose her singing voice when she was only 35. She divorced her husband to be with her boyfriend, the millionaire Aristotle Onassis. But Onassis did not marry her. He married Jacqueline Kennedy. Maria Callas died in 1977 at the age of 53. We remember her as one of the greatest opera singers of the twentieth century.

VOCABULARY

◆ MEANING

Write the correct words in the blanks.

forced	contest	argued	lied
permanent	emotion	throat	

1. Maria's mother did not tell the truth about Maria's age. She _____.

2. Maria did not want to sing. Her mother said she must. Her mother _____ her to sing.

3. Callas became part of the National Opera for the rest of her life. She became a _____ member.

4. The front part of your neck is your _____.

5. Maria's parents _____. They had fights using loud, angry words.

6. Callas showed her feelings when she sang. She sang with great _____.

7. A _____ is a competition where people try to win a prize.

◆ USE

Work with a partner to answer these questions. Use complete sentences.

1. What were you *forced* to do as a child? How did you feel about it?

2. What kind of *contest* do you think you could win?

3. Who do you *argue* with?

4. When does a person show a lot of *emotion?*

5. When does your *throat* hurt?

COMPREHENSION

◆ UNDERSTANDING THE READING

Circle the letter of the correct answer.

1. As a child Callas had a _____.

   a. happy life   b. special voice   c. lot of friends

2. Elvira de Hidalgo helped Callas _____.

   a. pay for expensive   b. lie about her age   c. join Greece's National
       lessons   Opera

3. Callas became famous because she _____.

   a. sang with strong   b. had a famous   c. was a member of the
       feeling   boyfriend   National Opera

◆ REMEMBERING DETAILS

Reread the passage and answer the questions.

1. Where was Callas born?

2. What did her mother force her to do?

3. Which country did Callas and her mother go back to?

4. What did Elvira de Hidalgo teach Callas?

5. How old was Callas when she became a permanent member of the Greek National Opera?

6. What did some people call Callas's voice?

◆ UNDERSTANDING THE SEQUENCE

Which happened first? Write 1 on the line. Which happened second? Write 2 on the line.

1. _____ Callas went to the Athens Conservatory.
   _____ Callas sang at contests and on radio programs.

2. _____ Callas learned how to sing and act.
   _____ Callas studied with Elvira de Hidalgo.

3. _____ Callas gave 50 performances a year.
   _____ Callas became a permanent member of Greece's National Opera.

4. _____ Callas divorced her husband.
   _____ Aristotle Onassis married Jacqueline Kennedy.

◆ TELL THE STORY

Work with a partner. Tell the story of Maria Callas to your partner. Use your own words. Your partner can ask you questions about the story. Then, your partner tells you the story and you ask questions.

DISCUSSION

Discuss the answers to these questions with your classmates.

1. Should parents force their children to enter contests? Why or why not?

2. There are rich and famous people who are not happy. Which is more important: to be happy or to be rich and famous?

3. Which singer do you think has a "golden voice" today?

WRITING

Write about what kind of music is popular in your country. Who is your favorite singer?

Example: *In my country young people listen to pop music. My favorite singer is . . .*

_____

_____

_____

_____

UNIT 16

CÉSAR CHÁVEZ
(1927–1993)

BEFORE YOU READ

César Chávez was a farm worker. He helped farm workers get equal rights. What do you know about farm workers? Answer the questions with a partner.

1. What do farm workers do?
2. Do you think farm workers have the same rights as other workers?
3. Do you think machines now do work that farm workers did in the past?
4. Look at the picture of César Chávez. What can you say about him?

Now read about César Chávez.

CÉSAR CHÁVEZ

César Chávez was born in 1927 near Yuma, Arizona. His family owned a farm, but they did not have enough money to stay on the farm. So when César was 11, the family moved to California. They traveled to many farms to find work.

The Chávez family lived in work camps. The camps were terrible places. Often they did not have water for drinking and bathing. Often the family lived in a one-room house. Other times they stayed in a **tent.** They worked many hours in the fields. Sometimes the farmers **cheated** them. They paid the workers very little money. Most of the workers were from Mexico and did not speak English. They were afraid to say anything about the low pay because they did not want to lose their jobs.

Chávez saw these problems, and he did not forget them. He was intelligent. But he did not have much education. His family moved so often that sometimes he went to a school for only a week. Sometimes he went for only a day. He went to over 65 schools before he finished eighth grade.

Chávez was in the navy during World War II. After the war, he got married and got a job on a farm. There were problems on this farm, too. Chávez talked to the workers about their **rights.** The owners got mad, and Chávez's boss **fired** him. Chávez began to work for a group that helped Mexican Americans have better lives. Then he started a farm workers' **union.**

Chávez became famous because of his ideas. Chávez did not like **violence.** He helped workers in peaceful ways. Often he **fasted.** When he fasted, people noticed him, and then they talked about the workers' problems, too. The government eventually passed laws to protect workers and make their living and working conditions better.

Chávez died in 1993 at the age of 66. He had health problems because he worked hard and fasted for many years. He gave his life to help others. César Chávez was a great hero in the fight for equal rights.

VOCABULARY

◆ MEANING

Write the correct words in the blanks.

tent	cheat	rights	fasted
fired	union	violence	

1. César Chávez did not eat or drink anything for several days. He _____.

2. Chávez's boss told him, "I do not want you to work here anymore." His boss _____ him.

3. Some farmers do not pay what they say they will pay. They _____ their workers.

4. When people sleep outside, they often sleep in a _____.

5. Chávez told the other workers about the law. He told them what they could and could not do. He told them about their _____.

6. Chávez didn't like people to hurt each other. He liked peace, not _____.

7. Chávez started an organization for workers. He started a _____.

◆ USE

Work with a partner to answer these questions. Use complete sentences.

1. Did you ever sleep in a *tent?* Why? *yes*

2. Why do some students *cheat* on tests?

3. What *rights* do you have? Give an example.

4. Why do some workers get *fired?*

5. Do you think there is too much *violence* on TV? Why or why not?

COMPREHENSION

◆ UNDERSTANDING THE READING

Circle the letter of the correct answer.

1. As a child, César Chávez learned about _____ in the camps.
   a. workers' rights   b. terrible conditions   c. family problems

2. Chávez started _____.
   a. camps for workers   b. small farms for Mexican workers   c. a union for farm workers

3. Chávez was _____.
   a. not a farm worker   b. a peaceful man   c. from Mexico

◆ REMEMBERING DETAILS

One word in each sentence is not correct. Find the word and cross it out. Write the correct word.

1. Most of the workers from Mexico did not speak Spanish.

2. Chávez went to 65 jobs before he finished eighth grade.

3. Sometimes the farmers helped their workers.

4. Chávez's family went to Arizona to find work.

5. Chávez started a school workers' union.

6. Chávez was in the army in World War II.

◆ SENTENCE COMPLETION

Match the words in Column A and Column B to make sentences.

A	B
___ 1. The Chávez family went to California	a. speak English.
___ 2. The workers were afraid	b. to find work.
___ 3. The workers could not	c. because he worked hard.
___ 4. Many important people liked	d. to say anything.
___ 5. Doctors said Chávez died	e. Chávez's ideas.

◆ DICTATION

Work with a partner. Read four sentences from the exercise above. Your partner listens and writes the sentences. Then, your partner reads four sentences and you write them.

DISCUSSION

Discuss the answers to these questions with your classmates.

1. In your country are there workers who are not treated well? Who are they?

2. Who has helped to change government laws? Is this hard to do? Why or why not?

3. Should farm workers be paid as well as other workers? Why or why not?

WRITING

Describe your own workday or the workday of someone you know.

Example: *I take the bus at 7 A.M. to get to work. My work starts at 7:30.*

_____

_____

_____

_____

UNIT 17

ANNE FRANK
(1929–1945)

BEFORE YOU READ

Anne Frank was a Jewish girl. She died at age 15 during World War II. What do you know about World War II? Answer the questions with a partner.

1. When was World War II?
2. Who was the leader of Germany in World War II?
3. What did this person want to do?
4. Look at the picture of Anne Frank. What can you say about her?

Now read about Anne Frank.

ANNE FRANK

Anne Frank was born in 1929 in Frankfurt, Germany. Her family was Jewish. She lived happily with her parents and older sister, Margot. In 1933, Adolf Hitler became the leader of Germany. Then everything changed.

Hitler passed laws against Jews and other groups of people. They lost their jobs and were forced out of their homes. Many people were killed. The government sent others to prisons called concentration camps. Life in the camps was **horrible.** Millions of people died there.

The Frank family ran away to Amsterdam, Holland. They were safe for a while. In 1939, World War II started, and in 1940, Hitler's **army** came to Holland. Life became very bad in Holland, too.

Anne's father, Otto, hid his family in secret rooms in an office building. Another Jewish family hid there, too. Dutch friends brought food for them. Often they did not have enough food. During the day, they had to be very quiet. They lived in **fear.** They stayed there almost two years.

Every day Anne Frank wrote in her **diary.** She described her feelings and what she saw. Life was very hard, but she wrote about good things, too. On June 6, 1944, the two families heard important news on their radio. The armies of England and the United States were now in France. The war was going to end. Everyone was very happy.

Right before the war ended, someone **betrayed** them. The German secret police came. The police sent the two families to the concentration camps. Sadly, they were on the last train from Amsterdam to the concentration camps.

Anne's mother died of **starvation.** Anne and her sister died from a disease called typhus. Only Otto Frank **survived.** In 1948, he published *The Diary of Anne Frank.* Because of her diary, people all over the world know the story of Anne Frank.

VOCABULARY

◆ MEANING

Write the correct words in the blanks.

horrible	army	fear	diary
betrayed	starvation	survived	

1. Anne Frank's family hid for two years. They were afraid. They lived in
   _____ that the Germans would find them.

2. Anne's mother didn't have enough food to eat. She became very sick.
   Eventually, she died of _____.

3. Anne's father lived. All the others died. Only Otto Frank _____.

4. Concentration camps were _____. Many bad things happened there.

5. Germany had many soldiers. Germany had a big _____.

6. Anne had a small notebook. In it she wrote about her daily life. She wrote in her

   _____.

7. Someone told the German secret police where the Frank family was hiding. That

   person _____ the Frank family.

◆ USE

Work with a partner to answer these questions. Use complete sentences.

1. War is a *horrible* thing. What else is horrible?

2. Are there women in your country's *army?* Why or why not?

3. What do you *fear* the most?

4. Do you keep a *diary?* If so, what do you write about? If not, why not?

5. What would you do if your best friend *betrayed* you?

6. What should you give someone who is dying of *starvation?*

7. When you go camping, what do you need to *survive?*

COMPREHENSION

◆ UNDERSTANDING THE READING

Circle the letter of the correct answer.

1. Anne Frank and her family had problems because they _____.
   a. moved to Amsterdam   b. hid in an office   c. were Jewish

2. The Frank family hid from _____.
   a. the Germans   b. the Dutch   c. the English

3. Anne Frank is famous because she _____.
   a. was young   b. wrote a diary   c. was Jewish

◆ REMEMBERING DETAILS

Reread the passage and answer the questions.

1. What was Anne Frank's religion?

2. When did World War II begin?

3. Who was the leader of Germany during World War II?

4. Where did the Frank family go to hide?

5. Where did millions of Jews die?

6. Who published Anne Frank's diary?

◆ UNDERSTANDING THE SEQUENCE

Which happened first? Write 1 on the line. Which happened second? Write 2 on the line.

1. _____ Hitler was the leader of Germany.
   _____ World War II started.

2. _____ Dutch friends brought food to the Frank family.
   _____ Anne and her family hid in an office building.

3. _____ World War II ended.
   _____ The German secret police took Anne and her family.

4. _____ Anne, her sister, and her mother died.
   _____ Otto Frank published Anne's diary.

◆ TELL THE STORY

Work with a partner. Tell the story of Anne Frank to your partner. Use your own words. Your partner can ask you questions about the story. Then, your partner tells you the story and you ask questions.

DISCUSSION

Discuss the answers to these questions with your classmates.

1. Is it a good idea to put personal information in your diary? Why or why not?

2. Dutch people helped Anne Frank's family. Do you think they did the right thing? Why or why not?

3. What lesson can we learn from Anne Frank's story?

WRITING

Write a few lines about your day in your diary.

Example: *Dear Diary, Today I woke up late.*

_____

_____

_____

_____

UNIT 18
ROBERTO CLEMENTE
(1934–1972)

BEFORE YOU READ

Roberto Clemente was a great baseball player from Puerto Rico. What do you know about sports? Answer the questions with a partner.

1. What sports are popular in your country?
2. In which countries is baseball popular?
3. Who are some famous athletes in your country? What sports do they play?
4. Look at the picture of Roberto Clemente. What can you say about him?

Now read about Roberto Clemente.

ROBERTO CLEMENTE

Roberto Clemente was born in 1934 near San Juan, Puerto Rico. His parents did not have much money. But they taught their children to be good and **honest.** They also taught their children the importance of **honor.** Clemente had all of these qualities.

As a child, Roberto loved baseball. He listened to baseball games on the radio. He played baseball with his friends. He also played in high school on a city team. When he graduated from high school in 1953, nine professional teams wanted Clemente to play for them. The Brooklyn Dodgers offered him $10,000. Clemente said "yes." Then another team offered him $30,000! Clemente asked his parents for **advice.** His mother said that he must **keep his word.** So he signed a contract with the Dodgers. But he never played a game with them.

In 1954, he began to play for another team, the Pittsburgh Pirates. The Pirates were not winning a lot of games. But Clemente helped them get better. In 1960, the Pirates won the World Series Championship for the first time in 33 years. In 1965, Clemente won the award for the Most Valuable Player. In 1971, the Pirates won the World Series again. Clemente was named the Most Valuable Player in the series.

Clemente received many awards and made a lot of money. But he gave a lot, too. He gave to charities in the United States and in Puerto Rico. Every winter he went back to Puerto Rico and worked with children. He taught them about baseball. He also taught them about honor and honesty.

In December 1972, there was an earthquake in Nicaragua. Clemente collected food, clothing, and medicine for the people. On New Year's Eve, he went on a plane to bring the **supplies** to Nicaragua. But after the plane **took off,** it **crashed** into the water. Everyone on the plane died. Roberto Clemente was a great baseball player and a hero.

VOCABULARY

◆ MEANING

Write the correct words in the blanks.

honest	honor	advice	keep his word
supplies	took off	crashed	

1. Roberto Clemente often asked his parents for help. He wanted their opinion when he had a problem. He wanted their _____.

2. Clemente's plane did not come down safely. It _____ in the water.

3. The plane to Nicaragua was carrying things people needed for everyday life, such as food and clothing. It was carrying _____.

4. His parents told him to tell the truth. They wanted him to be _____.

5. Clemente's mother told him to do what he promised. She told him to always _____.

6. Clemente's parents told him to act with respect toward himself and others. They told him the importance of _____.

7. The plane _____. It left for Nicaragua.

◆ USE

Work with a partner to answer these questions. Use complete sentences.

1. Can you be *honest* all the time? Why or why not?

2. Who is a person of *honor* in your city or country?

3. What good *advice* did your parents give you?

4. Why is it important to *keep your word?*

5. What kind of *supplies* do people need after an earthquake?

COMPREHENSION

◆ UNDERSTANDING THE READING

Circle the letter of the correct answer.

1. Clemente was _____.
   a. a sports hero   b. in the earthquake in Nicaragua   c. born in New York

2. Clemente was named Most Valuable Player _____.
   a. once   b. twice   c. three times

3. Clemente gave money to _____.
   a. charities   b. baseball players   c. his mother

◆ REMEMBERING DETAILS

Reread the passage and answer the questions.

1. Where was Roberto Clemente born?

2. Which team did he sign a contract with first?

3. When did the Pirates win for the first time in 33 years?

4. What happened in December 1972 in Nicaragua?

5. When did Clemente get on the plane to Nicaragua?

6. What happened to the plane?

Which happened first? Write 1 on the line. Which happened second? Write 2 on the line.

1. _____ A team offered Clemente $30,000.
   _____ The Dodgers offered Clemente $10,000.

2. _____ Clemente signed a contract with the Dodgers.
   _____ Clemente asked his parents for advice.

3. _____ Clemente won an award as the Most Valuable Player.
   _____ The Pirates won the championship for the first time in 33 years.

4. _____ The Pirates won the championship a second time.
   _____ Clemente collected food, clothes, and medicine for the Nicaraguans.

◆ TELL THE STORY

Work with a partner. Tell the story of Roberto Clemente to your partner. Use your own words. Your partner can ask you questions about the story. Then, your partner tells you the story and you ask questions.

DISCUSSION

Discuss the answers to these questions with your classmates.

1. Why do you think Clemente is a hero?

2. Name some other sports stars who are heroes. Why are they heroes?

3. Can you think of sports stars who set bad examples? What do they do? How should they change?

WRITING

Describe a famous person from your country.

Example: *A famous person from my country is Simón Bolívar.*

_____

_____

_____

_____

UNIT 19

JANE GOODALL
(1934–)

BEFORE YOU READ

Jane Goodall went to Africa and studied wild chimpanzees for almost 40 years. What do you think she found out about chimpanzees? Are these sentences true? Check (✔) *Yes* or *No*.

1. Chimpanzees eat meat.   ○ Yes   ○ No
2. Chimpanzees are very similar to people.   ○ Yes   ○ No
3. Chimpanzees use tools to get food.   ○ Yes   ○ No
4. Chimpanzees have personalities.   ○ Yes   ○ No

Now read about Jane Goodall and check your answers.

JANE GOODALL

Jane Goodall was born in 1934 in London, England. When she was two years old, her father gave her a toy chimpanzee named Jubilee. It was her favorite toy. In fact, she still has Jubilee at her home in England. She also loved to play with animals and read stories. Her favorite stories were about Africa. Her childhood dream was to go there.

Jane went to secretarial school and then she worked for a film company. A friend invited her to Kenya, so she worked as a waitress and saved enough money for the boat trip to Kenya. She was 23 years old.

In Kenya, she met the famous **anthropologist** Louis Leakey. Goodall knew so much about Africa that Leakey **hired** her as his assistant. She traveled with him and his wife, Mary, to search for **evidence** of prehistoric man. Leakey and Goodall wanted to study chimpanzees because they were very similar to humans. Goodall did not have a university degree. But Leakey thought she was the **ideal** person to study chimpanzees.

At first the government did not approve of Goodall's work. It was unusual for a woman to live in the **wild** country alone. Her mother decided to go with her, so the government finally agreed.

In July 1960, Goodall began to study the chimpanzees. It wasn't easy at first. Every morning she went to the same place. After about six months, the chimps came near her. She gave each one a name, like a person. Goodall was the first scientist to do this. She thought that each chimpanzee had its own **personality**, just like people. One day, she noticed that the chimpanzees used **tools** to get their food. Scientists always thought only people knew how to use tools! She also discovered that chimps eat meat as well as fruit and plants.

Goodall was married twice. She also has a son. Her first husband was a photographer, and her second husband was the Director of National Parks. Both men shared Goodall's love of Africa and animals.

Goodall studied chimpanzees for over 40 years. She changed the way scientists study animals. Today she travels the world and talks about the importance of chimpanzees.

VOCABULARY

◆ MEANING

Write the correct words in the blanks.

hired	personality	anthropologist	evidence
ideal	tools	wild	

1. Louis Leakey studied humans. He studied their habits, their cultures, and the size and shape of their bodies. He was a famous _____.

2. Leakey paid Jane Goodall to work for him. He _____ her.

3. Leakey had ideas about prehistoric man, but he needed _____ to prove his ideas were true.

4. In a national park in Africa, you can see many _____ animals.

5. A knife and a hammer are _____. We use them to make things.

6. Goodall was the perfect person for the job. She was _____.

7. Every person has different qualities. He or she has a unique _____.

◆ USE

Work with a partner to answer these questions. Use complete sentences.

1. You want to be an *anthropologist.* What subject do you study in school?

2. What is an example of a *tool?* What do you use it for?

3. What is an *ideal* job for you?

4. What are two examples of *wild* animals?

5. What kind of people does a restaurant owner *hire?*

COMPREHENSION

◆ UNDERSTANDING THE READING

Circle the letter of the correct answer.

1. As a child, Goodall _____.
   a. wanted to go to Africa   b. had bad dreams   c. did not like animals

2. In Kenya, Goodall _____.
   a. studied Leakey   b. worked for Leakey   c. worked for a university degree

3. Goodall found that chimpanzees _____.
   a. do not eat meat   b. eat meat   c. do not use tools to get food

◆ REMEMBERING DETAILS

Reread the passage and answer the questions.

1. Where was Goodall born?

2. How did Goodall get to Kenya?

3. How old was Goodall when she went to Kenya?

4. Who did Goodall meet in Kenya?

5. When did Goodall start to study chimpanzees?

6. How long did Goodall study chimpanzees?

Match the words in Column A and Column B to make sentences.

A	B
___ 1. Goodall read stories	a. the chimpanzees.
___ 2. She went to	b. a son.
___ 3. She studied	c. about Africa.
___ 4. She had	d. as a waitress.
___ 5. The chimps used	e. Kenya.
___ 6. Goodall worked	f. tools.

◆ DICTATION

Work with a partner. Read four sentences from the exercise above. Your partner listens and writes the sentences. Then, your partner reads four sentences and you write them.

DISCUSSION

Discuss the answers to these questions with your classmates.

1. Would you study wild animals? Why or why not?

2. Some scientists use animals for experiments in laboratories. Sometimes scientists hurt the animals and they die. Do you think we should use animals for lab experiments? Why or why not?

3. There are fewer and fewer chimpanzees today. Why are chimpanzees in danger?

WRITING

Describe an animal you like or you know about.

Example: *Sharks are fish. They are very dangerous.*

_____

_____

_____

_____

UNIT 20

PELÉ
(1940–)

Before you read

Pelé is one of the most famous soccer players in the world. What do you know about soccer? Answer the questions with a partner.

1. Is soccer popular in your country? Where is soccer a popular sport?
2. Is a soccer ball different from an American football? If so, how?
3. Do you know any famous soccer teams or soccer players?
4. Look at the picture of Pelé. What can you say about him?

Now read about Pelé.

PELÉ

One of the greatest soccer players of all time is Pelé. He was born Edson Arantes do Nascimento in 1940 in Três Corações, Brazil. His first soccer ball was a grapefruit. He also used an old sock and filled it with newspaper. Pelé left school at a young age to play soccer and work to help his family. Later in life, he finished high school and college.

Pelé was only 17 when people started to talk about him. It was 1958. Brazil was playing in the World Cup soccer competition. Pelé had an **injury.** He didn't play the first games, but his **team** needed him. Then Pelé went on the **field.** Pelé **scored** the only **goal** of the last game, and Brazil won the World Cup.

Pelé played professional soccer for 22 years. He scored 1,281 goals—more goals than any other player in the world. He helped Brazil win three World Cup titles. Pelé retired from soccer in 1971. People all over the world **admired** Pelé. Presidents and world leaders invited him to their countries. Nigeria once stopped its war for three days to let Pelé play. His talent is very unusual. Doctors once tested Pelé to find out why he played soccer so well. They found that he had excellent eyesight. He is also very intelligent. Pelé liked to do math problems and play chess. He said these activities helped him play better.

Pelé is married and has three children. He likes to be with his family. He also plays the guitar and writes songs. Pelé cares about people, especially children. He gives money to help poor children. He never **advertises** for tobacco or liquor companies. He knows that he has a great influence on young people. Pelé once said that he wants to "unite people, never to separate them." He is loved and admired all over the world.

VOCABULARY

◆ MEANING

What is the meaning of the underlined words? Circle the letter of the best answer.

1. Pelé had an <u>injury</u>.

   a. was hurt   b. was sad

2. Pelé <u>scored goals</u>.

   a. won points   b. got medals

3. Pelé's <u>team</u> needed him.

   a. friends from his country   b. a group of people who play sports together

4. People all over the world <u>admired</u> Pelé.

   a. watched   b. thought highly of

5. Pelé never <u>advertises</u> for tobacco.

   a. tells people to buy   b. thinks about

6. Pelé went on the <u>field</u>.

   a. place where the winner stands   b. place where people play soccer

◆ USE

Work with a partner to answer these questions. Use complete sentences.

1. What other games do you play on a *field?*

2. Do you *admire* someone? Who is it?

3. Did you ever have an *injury?* What kind?

4. What is the name of a *team* in your city or country?

COMPREHENSION

◆ UNDERSTANDING THE READING

Circle the letter of the correct answer.

1. Pelé is _____.

   a. very intelligent   b. from a rich family   c. his family name

2. Pelé is _____.

   a. the greatest soccer   b. famous only in   c. not a good person
     player   his country

3. Pelé scored _____ in the 1958 World Cup.

   a. three goals   b. two goals   c. one goal

◆ REMEMBERING DETAILS

Reread the passage and answer the questions.

1. Who was Edson Arantes do Nascimento?

2. What game was Pelé famous for?

3. How old was Pelé when he first played for the World Cup?

4. What was Pelé's first soccer ball?

5. When did Pelé retire?

6. How many goals did he score in his life?

Match the words in Column A and Column B to make sentences.

A	B
____ 1. Pelé gave money	a. people.
____ 2. Pelé cared about	b. with his family.
____ 3. Doctors said	c. for 22 years.
____ 4. Pelé liked to be	d. to help poor children.
____ 5. Pelé played soccer	e. Pelé was very intelligent.

◆ DICTATION

Work with a partner. Read four sentences from the exercise above. Your partner listens and writes the sentences. Then, your partner reads four sentences and you write them.

DISCUSSION

Discuss the answers to these questions with your classmates.

1. Do you think today's sports stars are paid too much money? Why or why not?

2. Many of the great players in sports have retired. Some people think there are not great heroes in sports anymore. Do you agree or disagree? Why?

3. If you could play professional sports, which sport would you play? Why?

WRITING

Write about a popular sport in your country. Describe the sport and sports stars.

Example: *A popular sport in Japan is sumo wrestling.*

_____

_____

_____

_____

UNIT 21
MUHAMMAD ALI
(1942–)

BEFORE YOU READ

Muhammad Ali is one of the world's most famous boxers. What do you know about him? Are these sentences true? Check (✔) *Yes* or *No*.

1. Muhammad Ali is an African-American.   ○ Yes   ○ No
2. Muhammad Ali is his original name.   ○ Yes   ○ No
3. Muhammad Ali continues to box to this day.   ○ Yes   ○ No
4. Muhammad Ali was "the greatest" boxer.   ○ Yes   ○ No

Now read about Muhammad Ali and check your answers.

MUHAMMAD ALI

In 1954, a shy boy named Cassius Clay, Jr., learned to box at a gym in Louisville, Kentucky. He was only 12 years old. At the gym, he met a **trainer** who taught him to move with light, quick steps. Cassius had a natural talent for boxing. With his **skills** and good training, he quickly became a champion.

In 1959, Clay won the National Golden Gloves **title.** The next year, he won an Olympic gold medal and became a professional boxer. Clay believed in himself. His famous words were "I am the greatest!" He told everyone that he was going to be champion of the world. Cassius Clay got a lot of attention. He wanted to use his **fame** to help get more rights for African-Americans.

In 1964, Clay became heavyweight champion of the world. Then he changed his **faith** and became a Muslim. He also changed his name to Muhammad Ali. In 1967, Ali refused to go into the army and fight in the Vietnam War. He said his reasons were religious. The World Boxing Association took away his title. They said that he could not box in the United States again.

Years later, the people in the association changed their minds. They **allowed** him to come back to fight in the ring. In 1974, Ali became champion again. He was the only man to be champion three times. Everyone in the world knew about Muhammad Ali. Everyone agreed that Ali was the greatest.

Eventually, Ali began to slow down. He lost his title to other boxers. In the 1980s, Ali told the world that he had a brain disease called Parkinson's disease. Now it is hard for him to speak and to use his arms and legs. But he still works for many charities. Ali likes to help young people in his town. He also travels all over the world to talk about human rights. He is a true hero of his time.

VOCABULARY

◆ MEANING

Write the correct words in the blanks.

trainer	skills	titles
faith	allowed	fame

1. Muhammad Ali learned how to be good at boxing. He learned all the necessary

   _____.

2. Ali belongs to the Muslim _____.

3. People who are well known have _____.

4. A _____ is a person who teaches sports.

5. The association said Ali could not box in the United States for a while. They said

   he was not _____ to box.

6. Ali won the championship three times. He won three boxing _____.

◆ USE

Work with a partner to answer these questions. Use complete sentences.

1. What sports use *trainers?*

2. What *skills* do you need to learn English?

3. Ali won the Golden Gloves title. What are some other kinds of *titles?*

4. Would you like to have *fame?* Why or why not?

5. What *faith* do most of the people in your country belong to?

6. What were you not *allowed* to do when you were younger?

COMPREHENSION

◆ UNDERSTANDING THE READING

Circle the letter of the correct answer.

1. Ali was the only boxer to _____.

   a. get an Olympic   b. fight for his faith   c. be champion
      gold medal   three times

2. The World Boxing Association took away Ali's title because he _____.

   a. was Muslim   b. changed his name   c. didn't want to fight in the war

3. Today Ali still _____.

   a. boxes   b. helps people   c. is the world champion

◆ REMEMBERING DETAILS

Reread the passage and answer the questions.

1. What did Clay win at the Olympics?

2. Who did Clay believe in?

3. When did Clay first become heavyweight champion of the world?

4. What did he change his name to?

5. What war did Muhammad Ali refuse to fight in?

6. What are his famous words?

7. What disease does Ali have?

◆ UNDERSTANDING THE SEQUENCE

Which happened first? Write 1 on the line. Which happened second? Write 2 on the line.

1. _____ Clay won a gold medal at the Olympics.
   _____ Clay won the National Golden Gloves title.

2. _____ Clay became heavyweight champion of the world.
   _____ Clay changed his faith.

3. _____ Clay changed his name.
   _____ Ali refused to fight in the Vietnam War.

4. _____ Ali became champion again.
   _____ The World Boxing Association took away Ali's title.

◆ TELL THE STORY

Work with a partner. Tell the story of Muhammad Ali to your partner. Use your own words. Your partner can ask you questions about the story. Then, your partner tells you the story and you ask questions.

DISCUSSION

Discuss the answers to these questions with your classmates.

1. Do you like boxing? Why or why not?

2. When do you think a sports star should stop playing sports?

3. Many famous people do work for charities. If you were famous, which charity would you help?

WRITING

Describe a sport you like to watch or play.

Example: *I like to watch ice skating.*

_____

_____

_____

_____

UNIT 22

ANITA RODDICK
(1942–)

BEFORE YOU READ

Anita Roddick started The Body Shop. She sells beauty products made from natural things. What do you know about natural products? Answer the questions with a partner.

1. What natural products can you use for good skin?
2. What natural products can you use on your hair?
3. Why are natural products popular?
4. Look at the picture of Anita Roddick. What can you say about her?

Now read about Anita Roddick.

ANITA RODDICK

Anita Roddick was always different. She didn't follow everyone else. She had her own ideas. When she was in high school, she wanted to wear makeup. But she did not have money. So Anita used **ashes** as eye color. She used mayonnaise to make her hair shine. Anita made **cosmetics** from natural things. Later on, she did it again. Only this time it made her rich!

She was born Anita Perella in 1944 in Littlehampton, England. Anita became a teacher and taught for a year. Then she worked for the United Nations and traveled around the world. In 1970, she married Gordon Roddick. They had two children. Gordon also loved to travel. He decided that he wanted to ride a horse from Argentina to New York. Anita Roddick needed money while he was away. She decided to open a cosmetics shop.

Roddick found a shop in Brighton, England. The rent was very cheap. The store smelled and the roof **leaked.** Anita washed the walls many times. But they were still **damp** and green. They still smelled, too. So she painted the walls green. She filled the shop with flowers and perfume. She called it The Body Shop. It opened March 27, 1976.

Roddick made the cosmetics herself. She used **ingredients** such as plants, honey, cucumber, and other natural things. She also **poured** strawberry oil in front of her shop so people would follow the smell into her store. They did. People loved her products. The shop was a big success. Soon Roddick opened another shop. It was painted green, of course.

A year later, Gordon Roddick returned home. The Roddicks worked day and night, and the two shops were very successful. Anita Roddick traveled to many different countries. She talked to women about health and beauty. She used many of their ideas in her cosmetics. Soon, The Body Shop had stores all over the world. Maybe there's one near you.

VOCABULARY

◆ MEANING

Write the correct words in the blanks.

cosmetics   ashes   leaked

ingredients   poured   damp

1. Anita Roddick used honey, cucumber, and other things to make her products. She used natural _____.

2. _____ are the gray dust you get after something is burned.

3. The roof of Roddick's shop had a hole, and water came through it. The roof _____.

4. The walls were still a little bit wet. They were _____.

5. Roddick made products to make women look and feel better. She made

   _____ .

6. Roddick _____ the oil from the bottle of strawberry oil.

◆ USE

Work with a partner to answer these questions. Use complete sentences.

1. What is one thing you can buy in a *cosmetics* store?

2. What is something that burns and makes *ashes?*

3. What do you do when your tire *leaks* air?

4. What are some *ingredients* in a cake?

5. Why did Anita *pour* strawberry oil in front of her store?

COMPREHENSION

◆ UNDERSTANDING THE READING

Circle the letter of the correct answer.

1. Roddick made _____ .

   a. mayonnaise   b. cosmetics   c. natural things

2. Roddick used _____ ingredients.

   a. natural   b. cheap   c. typical

3. The Body Shop became famous _____ .

   a. only in England   b. only in America   c. all over the world

◆ REMEMBERING DETAILS

One word in each sentence is not correct. Find the word and cross it out. Write the correct word.

1. Anita Roddick painted the walls of her store blue.

2. She filled the shop with fruits and perfume.

3. She used ashes as hair color.

4. Gordon Roddick wanted to ride from California to New York.

5. The Roddicks had three children.

6. Anita Roddick was born in Argentina.

Match the words in Column A and Column B to make sentences.

A	B
___ 1. Roddick studied to be a teacher and	a. painted them green.
___ 2. Roddick got married in 1970 and	b. helped Anita in the store.
___ 3. Roddick washed the walls of her store and	c. had two children.
___ 4. Roddick traveled and	d. taught for one year.
___ 5. Gordon came home and	e. talked to women everywhere.

◆ DICTATION

Work with a partner. Read four sentences from the exercise above. Your partner listens and writes the sentences. Then, your partner reads four sentences and you write them.

DISCUSSION

Discuss the answers to these questions with your classmates.

1. What beauty secrets do you know?

2. Why do you think Anita Roddick was so successful?

3. Do you use natural medicines when you are sick? Why or why not?

WRITING

Write about your favorite store. What products can you buy there?

Example: *My favorite shop is the Farmer's Market. I buy my vegetables there.*

_____

_____

_____

_____

UNIT 23

MAYA LIN

(1959–)

BEFORE YOU READ

Maya Lin is an architect. She designed a famous wall in Washington, D.C. When people go to the wall, they remember those who died in the Vietnam War. The wall is a monument. We visit monuments when we travel to different places. What do you know about monuments around the world? Answer the questions with a partner.

1. What is a famous monument in Europe or Asia?
2. What is a famous monument in the United States?
3. Who do you think visits the monument in Washington, D.C.?
4. Look at the picture of Maya Lin. What can you say about her?

Now read about Maya Lin.

MAYA LIN

Maya Lin's most famous work is the Vietnam **Veterans** Memorial in Washington, D.C. It is a **monument** in honor of the people who died in the Vietnam War. Maya was very young when she designed it. She was an average American college student. Now she is famous for her monuments. Each monument tells a story and brings peace to visitors who see it.

Maya Lin was born in 1959 in Athens, Ohio. Her parents were from China. They were both professors. Her father was an artist, and her mother was a poet. Maya was a very intelligent child. She loved reading, math, and art. She went to Yale University and studied architecture.

In 1980, the U.S. government held a contest to find a designer for the Vietnam Veterans Memorial. Lin's professor asked his students to send in their designs. Over 1,400 artists entered the contest. There were no names on the designs. On May 6, 1981, the judges **announced** that Maya Lin won the contest. Her design was very simple. It was two long, black stone walls, which came together in a "V." The names of over 58,000 people who died in the Vietnam War were **engraved** on the wall.

Many people did not like Maya Lin's design. They wanted something more **traditional.** Some people were angry because the designer was a woman, and she was Chinese American! Lin was very hurt. Finally, the judges agreed to put a traditional monument near the entrance of the memorial.

But most people love the memorial. Thousands of people come to look for the names of their loved ones. They touch the names. They leave flowers and letters. They find peace there.

Maya Lin has continued her work. For example, she made a **sculpture** for the women at Yale University, and she designed a clock for Pennsylvania Station in New York. Maya Lin is one of the most important artists in the United States today.

VOCABULARY

◆ MEANING

Write the correct words in the blanks.

| veterans | monument | engraved |
| announced | traditional | sculpture |

1. People did not like Maya Lin's design at first. It was too modern. They wanted something more _____.

2. A piece of art made of stone or metal is a _____.

3. The judges told everyone who won the contest. They _____ the winner.

4. Lin _____ the wall with names of people who died in the war.

5. A _____ reminds us of some important person or event.

6. Men and women who were in the army, especially during a war, are

_____.

◆ USE

Work with a partner to answer the questions. Use complete sentences.

1. What does your country do to honor war *veterans?*

2. What is a famous *monument* in your country?

3. What kind of things do people *engrave* names on?

4. Who *announces* the winner in a contest?

5. Do you prefer *traditional* or modern design? Why?

6. What can you make a *sculpture* from?

COMPREHENSION

◆ UNDERSTANDING THE READING

Circle the letter of the correct answer.

1. Maya Lin is famous because she is _____.
   a. a female architect   b. the designer of   c. a successful Chinese
                        a memorial   American

2. At first people didn't like Lin's work because it was too _____.
   a. modern   b. boring   c. dark

3. Finally, people who visited the wall _____.
   a. felt sad   b. got angry   c. found peace

◆ REMEMBERING DETAILS

Reread the passage and answer the questions.

1. Where was Lin born?

2. Where is the Vietnam Veterans Memorial?

3. What country do Lin's parents come from?

4. When was the national contest to design the Vietnam Veterans Memorial?

5. How did Lin hear about the contest?

6. How many artists entered the contest?

7. How many names are on the wall?

◆ UNDERSTANDING THE SEQUENCE

Which happened first? Write 1 on the line. Which happened second? Write 2 on the line.

1. _____ Lin entered Yale University.
   _____ There was a national contest for the Vietnam Veterans Memorial.

2. _____ The judges announced the winner.
   _____ Lin designed a sculpture for the women at Yale University.

3. _____ Many people did not like Lin's design.
   _____ The judges put a traditional monument near the entrance of the memorial.

4. _____ People saw and touched the memorial.
   _____ People found peace.

◆ TELL THE STORY

Work with a partner. Tell the story of Maya Lin to your partner. Use your own words. Your partner can ask you questions about the story. Then, your partner tells you the story and you ask questions.

DISCUSSION

Discuss the answers to these questions with your classmates.

1. What memorials or monuments would you like to visit?

2. Why do you think the artists did not use their names in the contest?

3. Why do you think people liked the memorial after they saw it?

WRITING

Describe how someone who has died is remembered in your country.

Example: *In my country, when a person dies, we have a big dinner.*

_____

_____

_____

_____

UNIT 24

PRINCESS DIANA
(1961-1997)

BEFORE YOU READ

Princess Diana was always in the news. She was different from other members of the British royal family. How should members of the royal family act? Discuss your answers with a partner.

A member of the royal family should:

be fashionable	be warm and friendly	be traditional
get divorced	mix with ordinary people	be educated
be on TV shows	write a biography	have political opinions

Now read about Princess Diana.

PRINCESS DIANA

Princess Diana was born Diana Spencer in 1961 in Norfolk, England. She was the daughter of an **aristocratic** family. Her parents got divorced when she was very young. Then the Spencer children lived with their father. Diana went to a private girls' school in Switzerland. She returned to England and worked as a **kindergarten** teacher. Soon after, she started to date Prince Charles, who was a friend of the Spencer family.

Prince Charles and Diana became **engaged,** and in 1981, they got married. Hundreds of millions of people around the world watched the wedding on television. They had two sons, William and Harry. Princess Diana became the most popular member of the **royal** family. Wherever she went, the **press** photographed her. She was tall, beautiful, and stylish. Women wanted to look like Princess Diana. She became the most photographed woman in the world.

By 1992, the marriage had difficulties. Princess Diana and Prince Charles separated.

In 1995, Diana gave a famous television **interview.** She talked about her personal life and why she was unhappy. The royal family never talked about personal problems. The interview was unusual, but people liked the princess's honesty. In 1996, Princess Diana and Prince Charles divorced.

After the divorce, Diana continued her work to help people. She worked with the poor, with people who had AIDS, and with people who had drug problems. Everyone loved her.

In 1997, Diana had a **romance** with Dodi al-Fayed, an Egyptian millionaire. One evening they were in Paris. Photographers followed their car. The car was going very fast, and it crashed. Diana and Dodi died in the accident. It was August 31, 1997. She was only 36 years old. People all over the world were very sad about Princess Diana's death. They will always remember her as the "People's Princess."

VOCABULARY

◆ MEANING

Write the correct words in the blanks.

aristocratic	kindergarten	engaged	interview
royal	press	romance	

1. Someone who is _____ is connected to the king or queen.

2. Diana was from a rich and high-class family. Her family was _____.

3. Diana dated Prince Charles. Soon she agreed to marry him. They became _____.

4. Diana was a teacher in a school for children aged four to six. She worked in a _____.

5. The _____ was always taking pictures of Princess Diana.

6. Diana and Dodi had a _____. They liked each other, and they were dating.

7. Diana gave a television _____ and talked about her personal life.

◆ USE

Work with a partner to answer these questions. Use complete sentences.

1. Would you like to give a television *interview?* Why or why not?

2. What did you do in *kindergarten* or your first years of school?

3. How long should two people be *engaged* before they get married?

4. Who is someone from a *royal* family?

5. Who does the *press* follow a lot?

6. What famous movie star or sports star is having a *romance?*

COMPREHENSION

◆ UNDERSTANDING THE READING

Circle the letter of the correct answer.

1. Diana was the _____ member of the royal family.
   a. richest   b. friendliest   c. most popular

2. Diana's marriage was _____.
   a. unhappy   b. fashionable   c. private

3. Diana was called the "People's Princess" because she _____.
   a. was aristocratic   b. helped everyone   c. was beautiful

◆ REMEMBERING DETAILS

One word in each sentence is not correct. Find the word and cross it out. Write the correct word.

1. Diana went to kindergarten in Switzerland.

2. Diana worked as a photographer in England.

3. Diana was short, beautiful, and stylish.

4. In 1995, millions of people watched Diana's wedding on television.

5. Diana talked about her unhappy marriage on radio.

6. Dodi was an English millionaire.

7. Diana and Dodi died in a car accident in Egypt.

◆ UNDERSTANDING THE SEQUENCE

Which happened first? Write 1 on the line. Which happened second? Write 2 on the line.

1. _____ Diana worked as a kindergarten teacher.
   _____ Diana dated Prince Charles.

2. _____ Diana gave a television interview.
   _____ Diana and Charles separated.

3. _____ Charles and Diana were married.
   _____ Diana became very popular.

4. _____ Diana had a romance with Dodi.
   _____ Charles and Diana divorced.

◆ TELL THE STORY

Work with a partner. Tell the story of Princess Diana to your partner. Use your own words. Your partner can ask you questions about the story. Then, your partner tells you the story and you ask questions.

DISCUSSION

Discuss the answers to these questions with your classmates.

1. Diana's death was shocking news. Where were you when you heard the news? How did you feel?

2. Some people didn't like Diana. Why do you think that was so?

3. Photographers were following Diana when her car crashed. Do you think the photographers caused the accident?

WRITING

Write about a time when you heard some good or bad news.

Example: *Last summer, I was at home. My mother told me some exciting news.*

_____

_____

_____

_____

UNIT 25
WANG YANI
(1975–)

BEFORE YOU READ

At a young age, Wang Yani was a famous artist. Look at the picture of Wang Yani and her painting. Answer the questions with a partner.

1. What do you see in the painting?
2. How old do you think Wang Yani was when she painted it?
3. Do you like the painting? Why or why not?

Now read about Wang Yani.

WANG YANI

Wang Yani was born in 1975 in Gongcheng, China. Even as a baby, she loved to draw. She drew lines everywhere. She even drew on the walls! Her father was an artist. Yani wanted to be like him. So she tried to stand like her father as he painted. This made him laugh. One day, she painted lines on his painting. She was only two and a half years old, but her father got angry. She cried and said, "I want to paint like you!" Then her father thought about his childhood. He also wanted to draw and paint. But his parents didn't understand. They just got angry. He decided to help his daughter become an artist.

Wang Yani's father gave her paint, brushes, and paper. She improved very quickly. Soon her lines became flowers, trees, and animals. Other people liked her work very much. Her pictures were in an art **exhibit** in Shanghai when she was only four years old!

By age six, Yani had made over 4,000 paintings and drawings. She loved to draw animals, especially monkeys and cats. Her pictures had **bright** colors. They had a special style. They were **unique.** Her father did not give her art lessons. He even stopped painting his own pictures. He did not want his daughter to paint like him. He took her to parks and zoos to get ideas for her work. When Yani was eight years old, one of her monkey paintings was made into a Chinese postage **stamp.** Later, Yani started to draw **landscapes** and people.

Wang Yani's work was shown in Asia, Europe, and North America. When she was just 14 years old, she became the youngest person to have a one-person show at the Smithsonian Institution in Washington, D.C.

Wang Yani was famous at a young age, but she still has a **normal** life. Her parents never sold her paintings. So the Wang family lives like everyone else. Wang Yani went to high school and has other interests, like sports and music. But her art is still a great **joy** in her life.

VOCABULARY

◆ MEANING

Write the correct words in the blanks.

exhibit	bright	unique	stamp
landscape	normal	joy	

1. Wang Yani's paintings had strong colors. She liked to paint with _____ colors.

2. There are no other paintings like Yani's. She has a _____ style.

3. In Shanghai, Yani's paintings were shown in a public place. There was an _____ of her paintings.

4. Some people thought Yani had a special childhood, but she didn't. She had a _____ life.

5. Yani is very happy when she paints. Painting brings her great _____.

6. You should always put a _____ on a letter before you mail it.

7. The painting shows a view of fields, flowers, and hills. It is a nice _____.

◆ USE

Work with a partner to answer these questions. Use complete sentences.

1. What kind of art *exhibit* would you like to see?

2. Do you like to wear *bright* colors? Why or why not?

3. What is something that is *unique?*

4. Where do you buy postage *stamps?* How much does it cost to mail a letter?

5. Do you like to look at portraits or *landscapes?*

6. What gives you *joy?*

COMPREHENSION

◆ UNDERSTANDING THE READING

Circle the letter of the correct answer.

1. Young Wang Yani was always _____ pictures.
   a. selling   b. looking at   c. drawing

2. Wang Yani never had _____.
   a. a happy life   b. an art lesson   c. an exhibit

3. Today Wang Yani is famous, but not _____.
   a. rich   b. busy   c. happy

◆ REMEMBERING DETAILS

Reread the passage and answer the questions.

1. What was Wang Yani's father's profession?

2. Where was Wang Yani born?

3. How many paintings did Yani make by age six?

4. What animals did Yani especially like to draw?

5. Where did Yani's father take her to get ideas?

6. Where did Yani have a one-person show?

7. How old was Yani when she had a one-person show?

◆ SENTENCE COMPLETION

Match the words in Column A and Column B to make sentences.

A	B
_c_ 1. As a baby	a. had an art exhibit.
_e_ 2. When Wang Yani was two and a half, she	b. became a postage stamp.
_a_ 3. When Wang Yani was four, she	c. Wang Yani loved to draw.
_f_ 4. By age six, Wang Yani	d. had a one-person show.
_b_ 5. When Wang Yani was eight, her painting	e. painted lines on her father's work.
_d_ 6. When Wang Yani was 14, she	f. had made over 4,000 paintings and drawings.

◆ DICTATION

Work with a partner. Read four sentences from the exercise above. Your partner listens and writes the sentences. Then, your partner reads four sentences and you write them.

DISCUSSION

Discuss the answers to these questions with your classmates.

1. Imagine you could paint or draw. What kinds of things would you draw?

2. If Yani's father was not an artist, do you think she would be successful at such a young age? Are parents important for a child's success?

3. Child movie stars sometimes have problems later in life. Why do you think this is?

WRITING

Describe your parents. What do they do? What did your parents want you to be?

Example: *My father is a manager in a company in my country. My mother doesn't work. They wanted me to be a dentist.*

_____

_____

_____

_____

ANSWER KEY

Answers not given will vary.

Unit 1 William Shakespeare
Before You Read: **1.** No **2.** Yes
3. Yes **4.** Yes
Meaning: **1.** lucky **2.** disease
3. plays **4.** genius **5.** retired
6. twins **7.** poems
Understanding the Reading:
1. b **2.** c **3.** a
Remembering Details: **1.** 18
years old **2.** Stratford-upon-
Avon **3.** 37 plays **4.** *Romeo
and Juliet, Hamlet, Macbeth*
(any two) **5.** Stratford-upon-
Avon **6.** his family
Understanding the Sequence:
1. 2,1 **2.** 2,1 **3.** 2,1 **4.** 1,2

Unit 2 Louis XIV
Meaning: **1.** palace **2.** rule **3.**
powerful **4.** luxury
5. appetite **6.** fountains **7.** tip
Understanding the Reading:
1. c **2.** b **3.** a
Remembering Details: **1.** 72
years **2.** 17 years old
3. Versailles **4.** 1,400 **5.** the tip
of his nose **6.** the king and queen
Sentence Completion: **1.** c
2. f **3.** b **4.** a **5.** e **6.** d

Unit 3 Florence Nightingale
Meaning: **1.** nurse
2. respectable **3.** volunteered
4. lamp **5.** comforted
6. supervised **7.** profession
Understanding the Reading:
1. b **2.** a **3.** c
Remembering Details:
1. ~~wife~~ / nurse **2.** ~~Florence~~ /
Turkey **3.** ~~nurses~~ / lamp
4. ~~Elizabeth~~ / Victoria
5. ~~five~~ / two **6.** ~~43~~ / 90
Understanding the Sequence:
1. 2,1 **2.** 2,1 **3.** 2,1 **4.** 1,2

Unit 4 Emily Dickinson
Before You Read: **1.** Yes **2.** No
3. Yes **4.** Yes **5.** No
Meaning: **1.** ill **2.** garden
3. mysterious **4.** upset **5.** hide
6. publish
Understanding the Reading:
1. b **2.** c **3.** b
Remembering Details: **1.** F
2. T **3.** F **4.** F **5.** T **6.** T
Understanding the Sequence:
1. 2,1 **2.** 1,2 **3.** 1,2 **4.** 2,1

Unit 5 Peter Ilich Tchaikovsky
Before You Read: **1.** No **2.** Yes
3. No **4.** No
Meaning: **1.** composer
2. condition **3.** widow
4. contaminated **5.** offered
6. conducted
Understanding the Reading:
1. a **2.** b **3.** c
Remembering Details: **1.** St.
Petersburg **2.** Madame von
Meck **3.** 14 years **4.** money
5. 53 years old **6.** *Swan Lake,
The Sleeping Beauty,* or *The
Nutcracker* (any one)
Understanding the Sequence:
1. 1,2 **2.** 2,1 **3.** 1,2 **4.** 2,1

Unit 6 Marie Curie
Meaning: **1.** scientist **2.** rays
3. discovery **4.** graduated
5. treat **6.** award **7.** ruin
Understanding the Reading:
1. a **2.** c **3.** b
Remembering Details:
1. Warsaw, Poland **2.** Paris
3. a scientist **4.** radium
5. 39 years old **6.** 1911
7. Irene
Understanding the Sequence:
1. 1,2 **2.** 1,2 **3.** 2,1 **4.** 1,2

Unit 7 Madam C. J. Walker
Meaning: **1.** dirt **2.** fields
3. fortune **4.** product
5. charity **6.** mansion **7.** will
Understanding the Reading:
1. c **2.** c **3.** b
Remembering Details: **1.** F
2. T **3.** T **4.** F **5.** F **6.** T
Understanding the Sequence:
1. 2,1 **2.** 2,1 **3.** 1,2 **4.** 2,1

Unit 8 Albert Einstein
Before You Read: **1.** Yes **2.** No
3. Yes **4.** Yes
Meaning: **1.** wrinkled **2.** ordinary
3. physics **4.** principal **5.** mark
6. universe **7.** theory
Understanding the Reading:
1. a **2.** c **3.** b
Remembering Details:
1. a check **2.** Germany
3. because he didn't speak until
he was three years old **4.** 12
years old **5.** 1922
6. Princeton, New Jersey
Understanding the Sequence:
1. 2,1 **2.** 1,2 **3.** 2,1 **4.** 1,2

Unit 9 Pablo Picasso
Before You Read: **1.** No **2.** Yes
3. No **4.** Yes
Meaning: **1.** lock **2.** eventually
3. century **4.** studio **5.** candle
6. created **7.** drew
Understanding the Reading:
1. c **2.** b **3.** b
Remembering Details:
1. a painter **2.** Spain **3.** 8 years
old **4.** Paris **5.** 200
6. 91 years old
Understanding the Sequence:
1. 2,1 **2.** 1,2 **3.** 2,1 **4.** 2,1

Unit 10 Jean Paul Getty
Meaning: **1.** interest
2. kidnappers **3.** wealthy

4. release 5. refused 6. lent
7. stingy
Understanding the Reading:
1. b 2. b 3. a
Remembering Details: 1. oil
2. five 3. England 4. his
grandson 5. money 6. Malibu,
California 7. 1976
Understanding the Sequence:
1. 2,1 2. 1,2 3. 2,1 4. 1,2

Unit 11 Oseola McCarty
Meaning: 1. earned 2. relatives
3. humble 4. honors 5. gift
6. found out 7. generous
Understanding the Reading:
1. c 2. b 3. a
Remembering Details: 1. F
2. T 3. F 4. F 5. F 6. T
Sentence Completion: 1. d
2. f 3. e 4. c 5. a 6. b

Unit 12 Babe Didrikson
Zaharias
Meaning: 1. tournament
2. events 3. performance
4. concentrate 5. athletes
6. talented 7. chef
Understanding the Reading:
1. a 2. c 3. b
Remembering Details: 1. five
2. Babe Ruth 3. two 4. George
Zaharias 5. golf 6. 82
Sentence Completion: 1. f
2. d 3. a 4. c 5. b 6. e

Unit 13 Minoru Yamasaki
Meaning: 1. a 2. b 3. b
4. a 5. b 6. a
Understanding the Reading:
1. b 2. a 3. c
Remembering Details: 1. F
2. T 3. T 4. F 5. F
Understanding the Sequence:
1. 2,1 2. 2,1 3. 1,2 4. 1,2

Unit 14 Akio Morita
Meaning: 1. brand 2. brilliant
3. typical 4. generations
5. partner 6. quality 7. portable
Understanding the Reading:
1. a 2. b 3. a

Remembering Details:
1. Nagoya, Japan 2. *sake*
3. a small radio 4. the Walkman
5. because of the high quality
6. 1963 7. Mr. Sony
Understanding the Sequence:
1. 1,2 2. 1,2 3. 2,1 4. 2,1

Unit 15 Maria Callas
Meaning: 1. lied 2. forced
3. permanent 4. throat
5. argued 6. emotion
7. contest
Understanding the Reading:
1. b 2. c 3. a
Remembering Details: 1. New
York City 2. sing at contests
3. Greece 4. how to sing and
act 5. 17 years old 6. The
Golden Voice of the Century
Understanding the Sequence:
1. 2,1 2. 2,1 3. 2,1 4. 1,2

Unit 16 César Chávez
Meaning: 1. fasted 2. fired
3. cheat 4. tent 5. rights
6. violence 7. union
Understanding the Reading:
1. b 2. c 3. b
Remembering Details:
1. ~~Spanish~~ / English 2. ~~jobs~~ /
schools 3. ~~helped~~ / cheated
4. ~~Arizona~~ / California
5. ~~school~~ / farm 6. ~~army~~ / navy
Sentence Completion: 1. b
2. d 3. a 4. e 5. c

Unit 17 Anne Frank
Before You Read: 1. World War
II started in 1939 and ended in
1945. 2. Adolf Hitler 3. Hitler
wanted to kill Jewish people and
others that he considered inferior.
4. Answers will vary.
Meaning: 1. fear 2. starvation
3. survived 4. horrible
5. army 6. diary 7. betrayed
Understanding the Reading:
1. c 2. a 3. b
Remembering Details:
1. Jewish 2. 1939 3. Adolf
Hitler 4. Amsterdam, Holland

5. concentration camps
6. Otto Frank
Understanding the Sequence:
1. 1,2 2. 2,1 3. 2,1 4. 1,2

Unit 18 Roberto Clemente
Meaning: 1. advice 2. crashed
3. supplies 4. honest 5. keep
his word 6. honor 7. took off
Understanding the Reading:
1. a 2. b 3. a
Remembering Details: 1. near
San Juan, Puerto Rico 2. The
Brooklyn Dodgers 3. 1960
4. There was an earthquake.
5. New Year's Eve, 1972 6. It
crashed.
Understanding the Sequence:
1. 2,1 2. 2,1 3. 2,1 4. 1,2

Unit 19 Jane Goodall
Before You Read: 1. Yes 2. Yes
3. Yes 4. Yes
Meaning: 1. anthropologist
2. hired 3. evidence 4. wild
5. tools 6. ideal 7. personality
Understanding the Reading:
1. a 2. b 3. b
Remembering Details:
1. London, England 2. by boat 3.
23 years old 4. Louis Leakey and
his wife 5. 1960 6. over 40 years
Sentence Completion: 1. c
2. e 3. a 4. b 5. f 6. d

Unit 20 Pelé
Meaning: 1. a 2. a 3. b 4.
b 5. a 6. b
Understanding the Reading:
1. a 2. a 3. c
Remembering Details: 1. Pelé
2. soccer 3. 17 years old
4. a grapefruit 5. 1971 6. 1,281
Sentence Completion: 1. d
2. a 3. e 4. b 5. c

Unit 21 Muhammad Ali
Before You Read: 1. Yes 2. No
3. No 4. Yes
Meaning: 1. skills 2. faith
3. fame 4. trainer 5. allowed
6. titles

Understanding the Reading:
1. c   **2.** c   **3.** b
Remembering Details:
1. a gold medal   **2.** himself
3. 1964   **4.** Muhammad Ali
5. the Vietnam War   **6.** "I am the greatest."   **7.** Parkinson's disease
Understanding the Sequence:
1. 2,1   **2.** 1,2   **3.** 1,2   **4.** 2,1

Unit 22 Anita Roddick

Meaning: **1.** ingredients
2. ashes   **3.** leaked   **4.** damp
5. cosmetics   **6.** poured
Understanding the Reading:
1. b   **2.** a   **3.** c
Remembering Details: **1.** ~~blue~~ / green   **2.** ~~fruits~~ / flowers
3. ~~hair~~ / eye   **4.** ~~California~~ / Argentina   **5.** ~~three~~ / two
6. ~~Argentina~~ / England
Sentence Completion: **1.** d
2. c   **3.** a   **4.** e   **5.** b

Unit 23 Maya Lin

Meaning: **1.** traditional
2. sculpture   **3.** announced
4. engraved   **5.** monument
6. veterans
Understanding the Reading:
1. b   **2.** a   **3.** c
Remembering Details:
1. Athens, Ohio   **2.** Washington, D.C.   **3.** China   **4.** 1980   **5.** Her professor told her.   **6.** over 1,400
7. over 58,000
Understanding the Sequence:
1. 1,2   **2.** 2,1   **3.** 1,2   **4.** 1,2

Unit 24 Princess Diana

Meaning: **1.** royal   **2.** aristocratic
3. engaged   **4.** kindergarten   **5.** press   **6.** romance   **7.** interview
Understanding the Reading:
1. c   **2.** a   **3.** b
Remembering Details:
1. ~~kindergarten~~ / school

2. ~~photographer~~ / teacher
3. ~~short~~ / tall   **4.** ~~1995~~ / 1981
5. ~~radio~~ / television   **6.** ~~English~~ / Egyptian   **7.** ~~Egypt~~ / Paris
Understanding the Sequence:
1. 1,2   **2.** 2,1   **3.** 1,2   **4.** 2,1

Unit 25 Wang Yani

Meaning: **1.** bright   **2.** unique
3. exhibit   **4.** normal   **5.** joy
6. stamp   **7.** landscape
Understanding the Reading:
1. c   **2.** b   **3.** a
Remembering Details:
1. an artist   **2.** Gongcheng, China
3. over 4,000   **4.** monkeys and cats   **5.** parks and zoos   **6.** The Smithsonian Institution in Washington, D.C.   **7.** 14 years old
Sentence Completion: **1.** c
2. e   **3.** a   **4.** f   **5.** b   **6.** d

BIBLIOGRAPHY

Brill, Marlene Targ. *Extraordinary Young People (Extraordinary People)*. Danbury, CT: Children's Press, 1996.

Bryant, Mark. *Private Lives: Curious Facts about the Famous and Infamous*. London: Cassell, 1998.

Elwood, Ann. *MacMillan Illustrated Almanac for Kids*. New York: MacMillan, 1984.

Forster, Marcella. *Life Stories: Shakespeare*. London: Wayland Publishers, Ltd., 1995.

Hahn, Emma. *Unlikely Heroes: A Walch Super Reader*. Portland, ME: J. Weston Walch, Publishers, 1997.

http://www.brittanica.com. Chicago: Brittanica.com Inc.

Isaac Asimov's Book of Facts: Three Thousand of the Most Interesting, Entertaining, Fascinating, Unbelievable, Unusual, and Fantastic Facts. Edited by Isaac Asimov. Norwalk, CT: Hastings House Publishers, 1992.

Jackman, Wayne. *Life Stories: Anne Frank*. London: Wayland Publishers Ltd., 1992.

Krull, Kathleen. *Lives of the Artists: Masterpieces, Messes (And What the Neighbors Thought)*. San Diego: Harcourt Trade Publishers, 1995.

Krull, Kathleen. *Lives of the Athletes: Thrills, Spills (And What the Neighbors Thought)*. San Diego: Harcourt Trade Publishers, 1997.

Krull, Kathleen. *Lives of the Musicians: Good Times, Bad Times (And What the Neighbors Thought)*. San Diego: Harcourt Trade Publishers, 1993.

Krull, Kathleen. *Lives of the Writers: Comedies, Tragedies (And What the Neighbors Thought)*. San Diego: Harcourt Trade Publishers, 1993.

Lobb, Nancy. *16 Extraordinary Asian Americans*. Portland, ME: J. Weston Walch, Publishers, 1996.

Lobb, Nancy. *16 Extraordinary Hispanic Americans*. Portland, ME: J. Weston Walch, Publishers, 1995.

Louis, David. *2201 Fascinating Facts*. New York: Wings Books, 1983.

Marvis, Barbara J. *Contemporary American Success Stories: Famous People of Asian Ancestry*. Elkton, MD: Mitchell Lane, 1994.

The Oxford Children's Book of Famous People. New York: Oxford University Press Children's Books, 1994.

Pearson, John. *Painfully Rich: J. Paul Getty and His Heirs*. New York: McClelland & Stewart, 1995.

Reader's Digest Book of Facts. 3rd ed. Pleasantville, NY: Reader's Digest Association, Inc., 1995.

Rediger, Pat. *Great African Americans in Sports Series*. Calgary: Weigl Educational Publishers, 1996.

Welden, Amelie. *Girls Who Rocked the World: Heroines from Sacajawea to Sheryl Swoopes*. Hillsboro, OR: Beyond Words, 1998.